CW01501020

A Philosophy of War

Philosopher and writer **Frédéric Gros** is France's foremost editor of Michel Foucault's works and lectures. Gros teaches political humanities at Sciences Po Paris. He is the author of the bestseller *A Philosophy of Walking*, which has been translated into twenty languages.

A Philosophy of War

Why We Fight

Frédéric Gros

Translated by Gregory Elliott

VERSO

London • New York

Albertine Translation

This work was awarded the Albertine Translation Prize in non-fiction for excellence in publication and translation. Albertine Translation is a programme created by Villa Albertine and funded by Albertine Foundation

This English-language edition first published by Verso 2026
First published as *Pourquoi la guerre?*
© Albin Michel 2023
Translation © Gregory Elliott 2026

All rights reserved

The manufacturer's authorized representative in the EU for product safety (GPSR) is LOGOS EUROPE, 9 rue Nicolas Poussin, 17000, La Rochelle, France
contact@logoseurope.eu

The moral rights of the author and translator have been asserted

1 3 5 7 9 10 8 6 4 2

Verso
UK: 6 Meard Street, London W1F 0EG
US: 207 East 32nd Street, New York, NY 10016
versobooks.com

Verso is the imprint of New Left Books

ISBN-13: 978-1-80429-602-8
ISBN-13: 978-1-80429-604-2 (US EBK)
ISBN-13: 978-1-80429-603-5 (UK EBK)

British Library Cataloguing in Publication Data
A catalogue record for this book is available from the British Library

Library of Congress Cataloging-in-Publication Data

Names: Gros, Frédéric author | Elliott, Gregory translator
Title: A philosophy of war : why we fight / Frédéric Gros ; translated by Gregory Elliott.
Other titles: Pourquoi la guerre? English
Description: First edition paperback. | London ; New York : Verso, 2026. | 'First published as Pourquoi la guerre?' – Title page verso | Includes bibliographical references.
Identifiers: LCCN 2025031922 (print) | LCCN 2025031923 (ebook) | ISBN 9781804296028 paperback | ISBN 9781804296042 ebk
Subjects: LCSH: War (Philosophy) | Just war doctrine
Classification: LCC U22 .G75813 2026 (print) | LCC U22 (ebook)
LC record available at https://lccn.loc.gov/2025031922
LC ebook record available at https://lccn.loc.gov/2025031923

Typeset in Fournier by Hewer Text UK Ltd, Edinburgh
Printed and bound by CPI Group (UK) Ltd, Croydon, CR0 4YY

Contents

Introduction:
This Time, It Really *Is* War

The general reaction on the morning of 24 February 2022, following the invasion of Ukraine by Russian forces after Vladimir Putin's awful address, was one of shock.

In the preceding weeks, troop movements massing on the borders had been signalled. President Joe Biden had warned of an imminent attack, but no-one in Europe believed it. Seeing the long lines of tanks on the roads to Kyiv, people told themselves: it is a feint, a bluff in a game of poker. It was as if a war in 'bloodlands' already ravaged by twentieth-century history was quite simply *impossible*.[1] We know what happened next: the imposition of increasingly severe economic sanctions on Russia; what was intended to be a 'lightning' war on the Russian side got bogged down; territorial gains, certainly, but limited ones in the face of fierce resistance; Western support for the Ukrainian forces in their ever more outright and unified war effort; and then decisive counter-attacks, the 'official' Russian annexation of the occupied territories of the Donbas, and so on.

But let us return to the initial dreadful images of February and March 2022: jam-packed train platforms, mothers carrying children with vacant eyes, the tears of fathers staying behind to fight, while fragile little hands waved from carriage windows. Sometimes, photographers rediscovered the tragic beauty of black and white, and people queried when exactly these images dated from. Then others, just as terrible, followed: buildings destroyed, roads ripped up, motionless bodies on the streets, hasty burials.

Whether Italian or British, French or German, we were all grabbed by the throat, tormented by something obvious. We could all tell ourselves: this time, it *really is* war. More than a vague impression, it was a certainty. And we could confirm the metaphorical status of a bunch of expressions we were fond of employing bombastically: psychological warfare, trade war, generational warfare, and so on. This time it was war, but the *real* thing, at the eastern gates of Europe. The war we had sought to prohibit with the United Nations; the war we thought was the preserve of barbarian states; real war with its thousands of deaths, its widows, its orphans, and its cities devastated by bombs, advancing tanks, heroic resistance – that war was *back*.

First of all, we shall have to examine what conveyed such a strong impression of this 'return' to war, given that the last half-century has witnessed unprecedented forms of mass violence: proxy wars, guerrilla warfare, terrorist acts, global war, and so on. We need to begin by locating the current conflict within the bloody sequence of the last seven decades.

Yet it will be remembered – and we shall return to this reluctance – that Vladimir Putin refused to speak of war in his first address after the invasion. For a long time, he proscribed the official use of the term, referring instead to a 'special military operation'. But we are, after all, pretty used to such euphemisms: to characterize its foreign operations, the Western world has long referred not to war but to 'interventions'. But the obvious fact that grabbed us by the throat in February–March 2022 remained, and we were not to be deceived by hypocritical phrases: this time, it was indeed war – a *real* one. We need to go deeper into this conviction, to understand the power of this impression with the aid of all those thinkers – from Plato to Machiavelli, Hobbes to Clausewitz, Rousseau to Carl Schmitt – who have posed the question of war and attempted to define it. This inquiry focuses on a form, a nature, an essence. And to characterize war, we shall have recourse to a classic triad that will serve as a guide: the ethical, the political, and the juridical.[2]

A real war entails killing and dying in confrontation with an enemy, who likewise risks their life in order to kill. And this 'exchange' of death, this blood-stained reciprocity, involves what would today likely be called a 'moral' factor, in the elementary sense that judges and philosophers use the word, in straightforward contrast to the 'physical' – for example, fierce determination or unconquerable fear, heroism or cruelty, sacrificial courage or bloodlust, and so on. In any event, a real war assumes the solemnity of death – even if, during the Kosovo conflicts for example, the fantasy of a 'zero deaths' war (on one side, naturally) was briefly entertained.[3]

But real war is also the kind that pits states, peoples, political figures, collective entities against one another: it is Russia versus Ukraine, Vladimir Putin against Volodymyr Zelensky, Moscow against Kyiv, the Russian people versus the Ukrainian people, and so on. It assumes the operation of a binary principle that explains, and invariably entails, the temptation of Manichaeism: the good versus the bad, the brute against the innocent.

Finally, a real war is one offering 'reasons', 'justifications' and 'excuses', but also 'rules' and 'protocols'. Armed violence between states is supposed to be subject to laws, to respect rules and customs. Thus, in his initial address, Vladimir Putin made a point of justifying the start of hostilities by the alleged presence of Nazi elements in Ukraine, by the supposedly growing threat of NATO at the gates of Russia, and by the anti-Russian policies pursued in eastern Ukraine. We may regard these allegations as ridiculous or scandalous, but the main point is this: the obligation the Russian president felt to come up with them. War is never reducible to a pure balance of forces: it has to seem like a reaction to an *injuria* (an injustice), an infringement of rights: it is invariably presented as defensive, punitive, lifesaving. If not, reference will be made to savage raids, murderous pillage, sanguinary expeditions, but not to wars. Even colonial wars – which were only ever operations to get hold of natural resources, to brazenly exploit native populations – felt obliged to pass themselves off as 'civilizing missions'.

We thus have an initial tripartite divide, registered in one of the most famous definitions of war: 'war is an *armed*, *public* and *just* conflict'.[4]

There is one phrase that keeps on recurring in connection with the war in Ukraine. Whether anticipating the nuclear threat or denouncing the atrocious war crimes that mark the conflict, one concept is invoked either as a sombre, rather remote aura, or as the secret truth of armed conflict: 'total war'. We shall have to analyse this term to understand its implications as a conceptualization of violence.

This analysis of the profound nature, the eternal essence and the structural characteristics of war leaves unaddressed a question that philosophy cannot shy away from forever: *Why* war? To answer it, we shall have to call on psychoanalysis, sociology, anthropology, and so on.

Such are the six intellectual pathways proposed. Having followed them, we shall conclude with a final question: But war for the sake of what *peace?*

1

A Real 'Return' to War?

Binary Wars, Global Wars, Chaos-Creating Wars

In February and March 2022, during the invasion of Ukraine by Russian forces, a host of opinion-formers repeated in unison a phrase that recurred like a refrain: the 'return of war'. War, they sagely explained, had *returned*; an armed conflict of this kind had not been witnessed for more than half a century, since the 1945 armistice. So as not to lapse into ridiculous hyperbole, some were quick to add *on European soil* – which was to forget the terrible wars that marked the dismemberment of Yugoslavia, drawing a veil over the dead of Sarajevo, Srebrenica and Pristina.

Rather than speak of a return – a term suggesting that the war in Ukraine effected a *break* in half a century of peaceful European history – it is preferable to ask what *became* of war after 1945, and how the current conflict forms part of a series of major strategic changes that we shall present as a tragedy in three acts: Cold War, global war, chaos-creating war.

&

In the aftermath of the Allied landings in Normandy in June 1944 and the surrender, less than a year later, of Germany, followed by the explosion of nuclear bombs in Hiroshima and Nagasaki and the emperor's consequent announcement of Japan's capitulation, the great powers were struck by the immensity of the global disaster they had participated in. The macabre reckoning was due: tens of millions of deaths, thousands of cities and pieces of infrastructure destroyed, Europe bled white, and so on and so forth.

In retrospect, war seemed like an insane, absurd enterprise, and the great powers sought to establish means for prohibiting it, rendering it impossible.

More than a half-century later, can they be said to have succeeded? Analysts and polemicists have indeed referred to the 'end of war' after 1945 – but in order to claim that a particular *style* of war, the war that had structured the relationship between states, from the beaches of Marathon (490 BCE) to those of Normandy (1944), had given way to other forms of collective violence.[1] Pointing to this 'disappearance' was a way of saying that in the West the great powers, which had twice confronted each other during long years of insane, pointless destruction, had decided to do away with the idea that war is ever the *normal* way to settle a dispute between sovereign states, as implied by the great classical definitions: '*War*: dispute, quarrel between sovereign states or princes that cannot be ended by justice, and which is voided only by force, by way of arms'; or, again: 'the right of nations *to go to war* and to carry on hostilities is the legitimate way by which they prosecute their rights by their own power'.[2]

When the United Nations was set up in June 1945, it was 'to save succeeding generations from the scourge of war' (Preamble to the UN Charter). War between great powers that professed themselves 'major' and 'civilized' was prohibited; the international community sought to prevent conflict from starting. At the same time, war became 'impossible', but in a different sense: the apocalyptic power of nuclear arms would make it more like global suicide – planetary apocalypse at the mere push of a button – than a regular military confrontation. A few decades after Japan's capitulation, General Claude Le Borgne could write: 'war died in Hiroshima'.[3]

Yet this 'prohibition' (UN), along with this 'impossibility' (nuclear weapons), did not automatically bring about peace on Earth. Armed conflicts did not disappear, but simply *changed form*. When people speak of a return of war, it is actually to say that a certain *form* has returned, once again involving two sovereign states, presupposing deployment of armies, battlefields, aerial bombardments, military losses, mass exodus, terrified civilian populations, and so on. The Ukraine war must therefore be reinserted into the long history of the *styles* of war subsequent to the 1945 armistice – a history punctuated by shifts in the balance of power between the communist and capitalist blocs, wars of insurrection and national liberation in Africa and Asia, the terrorist attacks of the 2000s, and, finally, the chaotic turmoil in the Middle East following the Arab Spring – even if 'conventional' (territorial) conflicts persisted here and there, as between Iraq and Iran from 1980 to 1988.

The post-war period was geopolitically structured by the Cold War, also sometimes referred to as the 'Fifty Years War', consisting in a head-on clash between two blocs (the United States and the Soviet Union) representing two ideologies, two worldviews, two conceptions of freedom, two societal options.[4] Because each side possessed a crazy nuclear arsenal, on pain of plunging the world into an apocalypse the two mega-powers could not confront one another directly. So, war assumed less direct forms: a struggle to increase one's sphere of influence over third-party states; aid to one of two ideologically opposed 'camps'; 'low-intensity' conflicts. This was an era of 'proxy wars': each power supporting one of the parties within a proxy state, hoping to assist in its struggle and thereby impel it into a political embrace. These proxy conflicts were internal and binary, the triumph of one of the camps determining the nature of the future government (liberal or socialist). They could also take the form of the geographical division of a country, triggering a territorialized confrontation, as in Korea or Vietnam.

Such ideological conflicts invariably formed part of the extension of wars of national liberation, which was culturally conducive to the influence of the more spontaneously anti-imperialist Soviet bloc. Through them, peoples freed themselves from imperial tutelage (France, the United Kingdom, and so on). Wars of decolonization assumed another significance, this time strategic: they required of the occupied resistance forces a tactical creativity that led them to victory. Militarily, it was always David versus Goliath, the occupier possessing a modern army and greater firepower than the native populations – hence the description of these conflicts as 'asymmetrical' wars. Guerrilla techniques, already developed and applied in the previous century in Spain with the grinding down of Napoleon's armies, displayed their full capacity for destabilization. They meant exhausting an adversary psychologically without ever confronting it directly. The occupier was forced to fight a 'shadow army' which, concealed among the population, attacked isolated segments of the enemy army in occasional, savage, unpredictable fashion, creating a permanent sense of insecurity within it given its inability to distinguish between combatants and civilians. The insurrectionary principles of 'modern war' thus proved capable of foiling 'conventional' armies (those of the old occupying empires) with oblique tactics: outrages and sabotage, continuous harassment, surprise attacks, and so on.[5]

Symbolized by the 'fall of the Wall' in 1989, the dissolution of the Soviet bloc occasioned a first dramatic change in geopolitical history, signalling the end of the Cold War. Hopes arose for a period of hegemonic peace, guaranteed by the United States as world policeman. Such hopes even took the form of a hazardous announcement: the 'end of history'.[6] We were going to witness the triumph and indefinite extension of liberal democracy under the warming sun of the *Pax Americana*. The promise was short-lived. The attacks of 11 September 2001 delivered a fatal blow to the new utopia, indicating a new, more elusive enemy of the West. This enemy employed unprecedented, unpredictable tactical strikes, with diffuse political goals, directly threatening innocent civilians, and was organized through transnational networks without a fixed territorial base: fanatical Islamist terrorism.

The events of 9/11 ushered the post-1945 world into a second paradigm – what I shall call 'global' or 'diffuse' wars – that led to the collapse of the strategic reference points of previous decades. Within this new geopolitical horizon, major armed violence manifested itself in original forms referred to as 'terrorist acts', 'humanitarian interventions', 'counter-insurgency operations', 'preventive war', the 'global war on terror'.[7]

Obviously, the phenomenon of terrorism does not date from 11 September 2001. But hitherto it had taken the form of a desperate tactic against detested foreign occupying forces. Attacks were often targeted (security posts, symbolic sites of power) and, above all, accompanied by precise demands, often territorial. They always sounded like ultimatums. The 'classical' terrorist was (in Carl Schmitt's phrase) a 'telluric partisan': with the means at their disposal, they demanded complete restoration of their land, from which they were seeking to dislodge a hated invader by acts of violence.[8]

The terrorists of 11 September were not the same: they were a 'global' enemy. This was, first of all, because they possessed neither fixed national identity nor specific territorial anchorage, but also because they defended a cause that transcended specific political interests, and because they mainly struck civilians representing a despised way of life, a detested civilization, hated values. The attacks of 11 September signalled the entrance onto the stage of a global terrorism: comprising members of various nationalities, from the remote mountains of Afghanistan a jihadist network projected attacks that directly and indiscriminately targeted workers whose only 'crime' was to find themselves physically present in New York's Twin Towers, symbols of US power. At stake in global terrorism is something more symbolic than territorial – even if one of the motives invoked has been the presence of infidels on Islam's sacred soil. Above all, it involves punishing arrogance, avenging humiliation, eliciting astonishment, creating permanent insecurity. In it, violence also assumes a religious, purifying, mystical dimension: against apostates, infidels, heretics. The global terrorist attack stages an apocalypse before casting the impure into oblivion.

The global terrorist act – it would be reproduced in Spain, Britain and France – inaugurates a new geopolitical era. It eludes the structures of conventional wars, but also of recent proxy wars or other 'low-intensity' conflicts fuelled by the two blocs (socialist and capitalist). It pertains to a principle both of an indefinite extension of violence and the contagious spread of fear. Classic warfare manifestly works through a mechanism of concentration: each belligerent masses its armies at a given point and starts a battle whose outcome will determine victory. Spatially, war establishes conflict zones separated from peaceful zones. It thus involves generating ad hoc, and temporally and spatially limited, intensities of violence from which irreversible effects are expected, with a final division between winner and loser. By contrast, the terrorist act is a victory in itself: the very fact that it occurs, the event itself, betokens success. It is no longer constructed as a threat, an ultimatum or a warning, but as an instantaneous success by dint of its sheer execution, the violence it provokes, and the terror of civilians.

The reaction of the Western powers to global terrorism was twofold. In order to track the networks organizing the attacks, they instituted ever more intrusive procedures of total surveillance and comprehensive control that were increasingly threatening to public liberties. They gave rise to Edward Snowden's sensational revelations about the massive collection of data from wiretaps and internet surveillance in the United States. These intelligence practices further enabled targeted assassination operations. Because its target was an elusive enemy, a diffuse network, an anonymous organization, this global war soon felt the need to register tangible results and proclaim success: the equivalent of 'victories won on the battlefield' would be the assassination of the head of a network – a success that was illusory, since the dead man was immediately replaced by someone else. The sniper and the engineer piloting a missile-carrying drone became the new heroes of a war which, no longer featuring states as enemies, was compelled to embody evil in the form of individual criminals. With their method of attack, targeted assassination tactics had the additional advantage of reducing military 'boots on the ground' (such was the doctrine of 'counterterrorism plus' advocated by Barack Obama).[9]

The second reaction consisted in the development of military operations dubbed 'interventions', whose profile is irreducible to that of classic wars. For a start, they are presented as 'collective' decisions: UN resolutions, coalitions of states, NATO operations. They are never presented as a sovereign decision by one state against another, but are decided by a group of nations 'in the name of' humanity, international security, a new world order. It is now a question of striking at 'rogue states', denounced as facilitators of terrorism and providers of territorial bases for the training and formation of fanatical jihadists.[10] 'Intervention' is an ambiguous term, expressing the new geopolitical set-up: it pertains more to the technical, medical or policing sphere than to the military. To intervene is to restore an order, to reconnect flows. The paradigm switch is perfectly described by Pierre Hassner: 'the structurally pertinent notion replacing war as "continuation of politics by other means" is not so much deterrence (as during the Cold War), but *intervention*'.[11]

From a strictly military point of view, these interventions (in Afghanistan and Iraq) were successes, the crushing technological superiority of the 'interveners' being inescapable. The military goal (overthrow of the existing regime suspected of complicity with terrorist networks) was secured in a few weeks. But, once this had been achieved, the problems emerged. The international military operation led to the dismantling of national armies, and sometimes even police forces – all forces of order suspected of complicity with the former tyrants. A dizzying security vacuum was created, as in Iraq after the 2003 'intervention', which inevitably led to the development locally of an economy of outright plunder maintained by armed militias. Subsequently, violent conflicts of legitimacy soon broke out between religious communities and ethnicities to determine who would govern the country from which the old rulers had been driven. To cap it all, the new objective fixed upon by the international coalition ('nation-building' and economic reconstruction) was completely beyond the ability and competence of the 'liberating' armies on the ground. The very project of organizing accelerated forms of 'democratic governance' after driving out the 'bad guys', while attempting to choose the 'good guys', proved endlessly naive. The armies then fell back on organizing occasional 'sorties' out of their bunkers to neutralize pockets of terrorist resistance on the basis of intelligence – high-risk operations that inevitably brought with them blunders and catastrophic 'collateral damage', which soon made the coalition armies seem like occupying powers.

Such was one of the numerous paradoxes of this period of global war: the most murderous moments were not necessarily the 'terrorist acts' or the 'interventions' intended to respond to them (characterized by intensive air strikes preceding the despatch of ground troops). Peacekeeping became as dangerous as waging war. Here and there the fatal drift of security operations might be checked by applying counter-insurgency principles (under the inspiration, for example, of David Petraeus in Iraq), making it possible to gain people's confidence: greater immersion in the population, respect for local customs, learning cultural basics, and so on.[12] But the damage had been done. When the Americans withdrew from Iraq, they left a country torn apart by religious wars and prey to militias. As the last US troops left Afghanistan, the Taliban were already in the process of organizing their triumphal return, even though the Americans were supposed to have 'neutralized' them twenty years earlier.

The terrorist act and the response to it (the 'global war on terror') undermined a number of divisions that conventional conflicts had established. First up was the division between the internal and the external. Classically, as we shall see with Hobbes, internal peace and external war entailed one another: violent conflicts were situated on the periphery of states and protected a pacific heartland. Corresponding to the internal public order guaranteed by the police was the external peace ensured by the army. Further divisions structured classical war, such as that between combatants and civilians, whereby soldiers killed one another legally, even heroically, but the 'innocent' (etymologically *non nocentes*: not harmful) had to be protected from the fighting. In the global wars, unarmed populations become the first victims, and even priority targets. Moreover, the terrorist has all the appearance of a civilian until they set off their bomb in a crowd of people.

Another undermined division is that between peace and war, construed as two distinct states recognized by clear markers: declaration of war; signature of a peace treaty. Like 'peacekeeping operations', the terrorist act blurs the boundary between these two states, making them infinitely permeable. A final organizing division characterizing former wars was between the criminal and the enemy. In the terrorist act, the 'combatant' behaves like a criminal by killing people who are not facing death on the battlefield, but taking the metro, going to work, and so on.

Terrorism and the 'global war on terror' have largely exploded these divisions, as is once again perfectly summarized by Pierre Hassner: 'The distinction between war and peace, along with that between internal and external, public and private, state and society, the political and the economic, the national and the international, the transnational and supranational, loses much of its meaning.'[13]

This blurring would allow the Americans to construct the category of 'illegal combatants' and, after 11 September, to make torture for the purposes of extracting intelligence a weapon of war.

Obviously, there is no question of arguing that we have completely left behind the paradigm of global war (or 'twenty years war': from the attacks on New York to the departure of the last US troops from Afghanistan). Nevertheless, the endemic states of war that followed the major revolutionary episode of 2011 (in Libya, Syria, Yemen) reveal a new paradigm of violence in these devastated countries that we shall call 'chaos-creating wars', whose disturbing profile we must now characterize.[14]

With immense courage, the rebels of the Arab Spring denounced clientelist and repressive political systems in the hands of corrupt minorities. During the demonstrations, the demands were essentially democratic: separation of powers, freedom of expression, free and fair elections, the struggle against poverty. The rulers' response invariably took the form of brutal repression of opposition movements, leading to an inevitable radicalization and confessionalization of the conflicts, and soon to a terrible drift into civil war. To understand how chaos could so quickly come about, for example, in Syria or

Libya, we must recall that these countries were the fruit of colonial carve-ups in which each empire pursued its own exclusive interest (think of the Sykes–Picot Agreement), artificially amalgamating divided peoples. Liberation from imperial tutelage in the early post-war decades most often redounded to the benefit of autocratic regimes parading nationalist, socialist, and sometimes secular values, but characterized by an implacable authoritarianism resting on a clientelism organized around a family, a clan, or a religious minority (Alawite in Syria, Sunni in Iraq).

This deceptive nationalist and unitary façade, combined with practices of systematic plunder to the benefit of the ruling minority and ferocious repression of any opposition, explains why the spark of the Arab revolts could so rapidly degenerate into a state of chaotic war – all the more so given that foreign powers (Saudi Arabia in Yemen, Iran and Russia in Syria) joined in to support a particular community or faction militarily, sometimes invoking, to legitimize themselves, a 'responsibility to protect' (formalized at the time of the intervention in Libya under NATO direction).

Soon, the state as a framework for protection, a guarantee of security and stability *for all*, no longer existed. Already furiously criticized for its inability to construct a common good, now it simply displayed the face of a clique of oligarchs profiteering from oil revenues and other unearned income, willing to do anything to ensure their stranglehold on the national wealth – recruiting the armed forces that remained at their disposal to work exclusively to that end, without the minimal concessions that might have made possible some kind of public order, however atrociously unjust. Exploiting the general disorder, armed groups proliferated on the ground, extorting a terrorized civil society with promises of protection. Whether involving rulers operating on the basis of 'everyone for themselves' or savage militias, violence was used to the same end: ensuring immediate plunder, and extracting maximum profit from the chaos. For chaos is profitable. Whereas classical warfare was constructed as organized violence, in accordance with rules and depending on standardized and instrumental objectives, the chaos-creating wars, whose profile is visible today in Libya, Syria, Iraq and Yemen, are waged to maximize the profits of catastrophe.

A chaos-creating war is in effect waged *for its own sake*; it is not geared towards creating a peace. Violence is committed solely for its effects of immediate intimidation, terror and confusion. What soon prevails is the implacable law of arms, and civil societies – the ordinary people whose everyday life is haunted by the problem of how to keep their home habitable, to feed and care for their children – are taken hostage in a destructive spiral, condemned merely to *survive*. Nothing better illustrates this logic of chaos than Bashar al-Assad's liberation in 2011, when he felt overwhelmed by demonstrations against his regime, of hundreds of jihadists from prison to increase the confusion and break up any straightforward confrontation between democratic forces and the existing regime, deriving advantage from a chaos he thereby intensified.

The elemental violence released would assume a millenarian coloration, as we saw with the episode of Islamic State in Iraq and the Levant. The religious violence at the heart of the chaos-creating wars is millenarian in essence: it is purifying, promising the abrupt advent, without patience or mediation, of a definitive harmony, promising to separate infidels from true believers. It dreams of drastically changing time, making possible the immediate restoration, at the heart of the present, of an origin that has never existed and whose imminent return signifies the end of time itself. Religious millenarianism is, in its essence, catastrophist. For a generation *driven to despair by the present*, in search of meaning and enamoured of immediacy, it opens up a delirious promise of intensity: a 'sur-vival', in the sense of enhanced existence, and participation in turning history on its head, in reversing time.

Chaos-creating war, whose violence is both elemental *and* mystical, is the symbol and symptom of an insurmountable difficulty – our difficulty – in building a future. At the intersection of two incommensurable, yet strictly contemporaneous, dimensions of current violence (predation and millenarian mysticism), we find an inability to project oneself in time, to outline the shape of a reassuring future, to construct the present as patience stretching towards a better future. These new wars no longer serve to give birth to the future, as Hegel optimistically hoped when he witnessed Napoleon's troops passing at Jena: they strip the present of all its possibilities, realizing only total catastrophe. Chaos-creating wars generate space-times of continuous collapse, in which forms of survival are combined: the survival of a ruling minority at bay, building its power *against* civil society; the survival of populations condemned to pay dearly for their security day after day; and, finally, the 'survival' of fanatics finding in death – of others and of themselves – surges of existential intensification.

With the description of this third major paradigm, we can perhaps better situate and characterize the Ukrainian conflict. If it was so easy to invoke a 'return' to war, it was because in many respects the war definitely revives classical forms: flagrant aggression taking the form of a land invasion by conventional forces; fierce fighting in bitter defence of each plot of land, each town; a confrontation between two sovereign states, pitting two national armies against one another at vital points; precise concentrations of violence, punctuated by defeats or victories; the forced exile of vulnerable people (women and children). In other respects, however, we find elements of millenarian violence: the invocation by Russia of its mystical role in purifying European decadence; the exigency of a return to a mythical origin; the projected spectre of total catastrophe by means of the nuclear threat.

On the European side, by contrast, the Ukraine war restores the assurance – and this confidence is one of the elements explaining our support for the country under attack – that we are still *in History*, and that for some nations the European side can represent hope for the future. And if the impression of a 'return' to war can impose itself with such force, it is also because, in many respects (territorial invasion, deployment of conventional weapons, and so on), the conflict possesses a classical structure corresponding to the oldest definitions of war. It presents itself as 'armed, public and just'. Such are the three dimensions we must now explore.

2

Heroism and Barbarism

One day, Giacomo Trivulzio came up with this formula: 'To wage war, three things are required: firstly money, secondly money, and thirdly money.'[1] We must put the sentence in context: Trivulzio was a Renaissance war entrepreneur, a *condottiere* assembling and financing mercenary armies that he marketed and sold to the highest bidder for 'political coups'.

It is true that the cost of war is always astounding – often much higher than the economic profit the aggressors can bank on. This was made plain once again in spring 2022 with announcements by Europe and the United States of the 'unblocking' of billions of euros and dollars to supply Ukrainian forces with military matériel. So dependent is war on money that victory might seem guaranteed to those prepared to invest the most wealth to secure it.

However, historical counterexamples to this verity have never been wanting. The Americans' crushing material superiority did not prevent their disastrous, ruinous defeat in Vietnam. Both experts and actors in warfare have consistently denounced the inadequacy of a rather trite claim – to wit, the largest army always wins – and foregrounded what used to be called 'moral forces'. I am referring to the ethical commitment, the spiritual energy, the *desire* harnessed in fighting (to attack or defend, to riposte or destroy), the moral quality of the belligerent willpower.

This remark might seem curious, given that, for us, war has become synonymous with barbarism, atrocious savagery. But reading the texts compels us to recognize that the experience of war, from the beaches of Marathon to those of Normandy, has entailed a formidable matrix of virtues. The key term in Western ethics (virtue – *aretê* in Greek, *virtus* in Latin) refers etymologically to the soldier's courage and determination. Moral *value* has the same root as military *valour*. Moreover, war is saturated with ethical figures: the loyal, gallant knight; the freedom-loving citizen-soldier ready to die for the homeland, and so on. But is this not an idealized, sublimated warfare? Or, rather, in order to make war a moral experience, do we not have to assume forms of combat in which it is not yet technological competence that prevails, but investment of a life?

Yet for centuries war has been viewed as a laboratory of virtues, at the same time, and conversely, it has constantly been denounced as the brutal moment of reversion to a primitive bestiality, a resurgence of archaic instincts. The warrior can exhibit inhuman savagery as well as heroic courage. Paradox, ambiguity, contradiction: from a moral standpoint, war is bipolar. War is a moment of the exaltation *and* the breakdown of morality, a point of moral upsurge *and* debacle. It is certainly possible, and sometimes legitimate, to resolve the contradiction by dividing the belligerents in accordance with this duality, as is tirelessly repeated in connection with the Ukrainian conflict. Barbaric, bloodthirsty Russians will be contrasted with heroic, tenacious Ukrainians. The dualism is the more defensible and credible in that it involves a contrast between forces of aggression comprising soldiers and mercenaries and defence forces predominantly composed of citizens of both sexes fighting for their territory and autonomy.

We shall return to the accursed subject of the will to war in Chapter 6 ('Why War?'), where I will focus on psychological motivation: ineradicable cruelty, death instinct, atavistic aggressiveness, and so on. Meanwhile, we may search for the brighter side, and enumerate the self-evident ethical elements that have likewise always pertained to war, even if we must admit that they have become obscured with the increasing technologization of military methods. Since their invention, firearms have posed a problem: death is dealt from a distance, and can take the enemy by surprise. That is why, in ancient armies, archers had a bad reputation: undisturbed, they killed from sheltered posts. For example, the bow and crossbow were banned in 1139 by the second Lateran Council, at least as regards 'wars between Christians'. What was being condemned was death that struck through treachery, which was not the outcome of an *equal, open* confrontation. In this respect, the First World War (1914–18) represented a massive turning point: on display in its hopelessness was the end of war as a possible moral experience. Bravery, valour, a sense of honour – how could they be displayed in the face of shells and bursts of machine-gun fire? At the blow of a whistle, the infantry were compelled to quit their trenches and run, lining up like fairground targets. The statistics of the Somme offensive between July and November 1916 are staggering, intolerable: on the opening day of 1 July alone, tens of thousands of deaths. More than a million wounded and dead in all, to enable the Allies to gain ten kilometres. With rifles and shells, war had become a shapeless, anonymous 'great butchery' which, far removed from heroic reveries, could inspire nothing but the disillusioned cynicism of a Céline.

But let us go back to the time before this point of rupture, in order to understand what, for centuries, made war something that generated moral values. I recall our astonishment in February–March 2022: 'This time, it *really is* war.' If this obvious fact impressed itself with intensity on screens and in our consciousness, it was because outlined in the conflict, with horrifying clarity, was the profile of death. Something *grave* was occurring. Unquestionably, we were no longer in the realm of metaphor, analogy or image. The talk was of ruins and corpses. The Middle Ages invented a formula for 'making war': 'embarking one's body on a deadly adventure'.

But it is not the presence of death as such that distinguishes war. After all, we also come across corpses in the settling of scores between rival gangs, in acts of violence by criminal psychotics, and so on. In war, however, death has a special configuration: it is conducted via a *regulated* – one might almost say 'ritualized'– *exchange*. Observing specific rules of engagement, two entities (armies) clash over time and in defined spaces. In war everyone threatens the other's life to the extent that they expose their own. 'Real' war requires this reciprocity in risking death. We can then immediately understand why forms of 'killing' that target innocent civilians, or even unarmed enemy soldiers, are condemned and regarded as 'war crimes'. Bombing private buildings is a war crime; gratuitous massacres are war crimes – and so on. In light of this, there is no need to point out that the bombings of Hiroshima and Nagasaki (to take but one example) could be denounced as war crimes, if we agree to set aside a context (total war) and a precise strategic objective (avoiding the heavy losses an invasion would have entailed, putting an end to the world war).

The most complete form of reciprocity in the exchange of death is glimpsed in the utterly idealized – legendary, one might say – version that saturates epic narratives: the combat of knights, from Homer's oral epics to the sagas of *Star Wars* via poetic evocations of Camelot. These narratives describe one-to-one duels, a pure clash of forces. Everything is played out in the full light of day, fairly, preferably in a clearing – an *open* space. It is all about respecting the adversary: the aim is to win victory over him, not to destroy him; to outperform rather than to annihilate him. There is not the least disdain for one's opponent: his value grounds mine. The fight thus feeds off the desire essentially to surpass *oneself*, in such a way as to draw even more energy from the resistance encountered. It requires great energy, unfailing ardour, vitality, *heart*.[2]

But there is a risk, invariably decried, of a chaotic explosion – the danger of allowing oneself to be carried away by the whirlwind of forces one unleashes. Murderous madness can erupt at any time. Such is the tragedy of Sophocles' *Ajax*: the myth of the mad knight. Erected against such chaos is the barrier of the narrative that sets limits. By this I mean that, when they fight, knights and old-style warriors look to human memory, hope to have a tale made out of their 'noble deeds', sculpt the form of their 'fine death', which will be their sole true victory, and thereby seek to limit the looming fury.

To fight is therefore to take heart for a dazzling act, to find in the power flow of confrontations a resource for testing and enhancing one's energy. This dynamic exaltation of war is very old, and it persisted for a long time. From the 'fresh and joyous' war that brings 'tears to the eye' vaunted by Jean de Bueil in *Le Jouvencel*, to the shared jubilation at the explosion of 'storms of steel' experienced by Ernst Jünger during the First World War ('when we collide with one another in a fog of fire and smoke, we are but one, we are two parts of a single force, fused in one and the same body'), combat has always beckoned towards existential intensities.[3]

But alongside, or even against, epic impulses, Greek genius in its democratic age conjured up the vigour of another ethical figure: courage − but now as the capacity to *stand firm*, rather than as ardour. Hence, perseverance and endurance instead of energy and frenzy. This ethical revolution was contemporaneous with a decisive military break. The Greek invention of the phalanx, which led to Greece's military victories over the Persian kingdoms, fostered the exaltation of Athenian citizenship. Hoplite tactics became established in the Greek army in all the city-states from the fifth century onwards.

But what were they? Countering an enemy army that sent its soldiers to the front in dispersed order (a confused juxtaposition of cavalry, infantry, archers, and so on), they involved aligning a compact wall bristling with spears, deep-set ranks of soldiers. With his left arm (the right arm held the spear), each combatant held a round shield (*hoplon* in Greek) that covered his left flank, with the other semicircle protecting the right flank of his immediate neighbour – while, logically, his own right flank was protected by the shield of his companion in arms.

When imagined, when visualized, a unit of hoplites (the phalanx) is a striking metaphor for solidarity and equality.[4] Perfect equality, because individuality counts for nothing in this device of war. Above all, it does not involve, as in the chivalrous model, 'making a name for oneself' through some dazzling act. That would be to imperil the cohesion of the whole. The strength of the phalanx consists in its united, collective, homogenous character. Consummate equality also because each soldier's virtue lies in being indefinitely 'replaceable' by another: if an infantryman falls, the one standing behind him immediately moves up to take his place to reform the line and close it back up. Impeccable solidarity, finally, because each hoplite protects a second even as he is protected by a third. Everyone is sustained by the courage of another. One no longer even fights *against* an enemy, but *for* one's fellow soldiers.

What ethical thinking retains from this device is intransigently *standing firm*. Because when the phalanx experiences the impact of an enemy attempting to break it up, the point is to stand firm, keep in position, hold one's ground. Socrates was recognized for having been exemplary when fighting as a hoplite at the Battle of Potidaea. Much later, during his trial for 'corrupting youth and inventing new gods', when the Athenian judges suggested he accept exile to allow him to save his life, he replied spontaneously: 'No, I shall keep my post in the city as conscience-shaker. It is what I learned when I was a hoplite: to stand firm when the risk of death arises, when danger is imminent.'[5]

'Standing firm' is the soldier's principal virtue. For weeks, it sustained the Ukrainian soldiers entrenched in the Azovstal steel plant in Mariupol, who finally surrendered on 16 May 2022 'on Kyiv's orders'. 'Standing firm' has proved essential in all the urban fighting that has punctuated the Ukrainian conflict. For missiles can be launched to paralyze transport centres or airports, to strangle cities and wear down the civilian population, but success is assured only when the invader's army enters the city under attack. Then, in the absence of immediate surrender, victory is won district by district, building by building. The time is past when, following a formal declaration, 'waging war' signified two powers assembling their respective armies so that they could confront one another on a plain, an open field, with each belligerent feverishly awaiting sunrise to fire the first salvo – a scenario that reproduces the fair duel on a vast scale. Modern warfare is urban: it is won in the streets. Thus, for every Ukrainian soldier or patriot holed up in their house, gun in hand, in Kharkiv or Kherson in spring 2022, the point was to stand firm for as long as possible. Unlike the ardour presupposed by an offensive, the ethical force of 'standing firm' derives from the fact that it is immediately defensive and requires an effort of the soul. When Saint Thomas contrasts defensive *sustinere* with offensive *aggredere*, he observes that, in order to 'stand firm', an effort of the soul is needed, whereas in aggression the soul lets itself be swept along by the body's sheer fury.[6] The moral superiority of *sustinere* fosters a major spiritual posture: self-control. After all, as Plato notes, to be master of one's desires and impulses means, on the occasion of a 'war' against them, not giving in to them.[7]

Once again, the moral ambiguity of war is extreme: it brings out in human beings both their accursed part (bloodthirsty bestiality, terrible cruelty) and their divine part (abnegation, self-sacrifice). The simplest resolution of this ambiguity might, as we have said, consist in dividing up the roles, a differential distribution of individuals. Thus, people have continued to amplify the contrast – all the more readily, given that the facts sometimes helped foster it – between a sanguinary Vladimir Putin, psychopathic tyrant, heedless of the fate of his people, thirsty for the blood of others, and an heroic Zelensky, exemplary in his determination; or again, between a Russian army composed of bestial individuals saturated with vodka, hatred and idiocy, and a patriotic Ukrainian militia of sublime courage.

Heroic engagement in war has always been a subject for literary celebration. For example, commenting on the Greek victory over the Persians, Hippocrates, La Boétie and Rousseau laid down an interpretive grid that we will find in connection with other battles: there were many more Persians, but the only thing they fought for was their pay, while, facing them, a handful of Greeks fought for their freedom, their history, their family. The energy displayed was all-conquering.

We shall find such images intact in commemorative speeches before monuments to the First World War. What is celebrated in them is the ability demonstrated by the soldiers to sacrifice themselves so that unimpaired freedom and an inviolate home-land survive beyond them. Such is the contrast between an oppressor motivated by tyrannical rage, represented by an army of slaves risking their lives only out of submission, and a civi-lized people wedded to values of justice. What the soldiers of freedom defend is also a certain national identity, represented by a history and a culture (a language, a religion, institutions, a cultural heritage), a way of living together, a community of values (justice, sharing, respect for rights, and so on). This ethi-cal ensemble is threatened by external aggression aiming to negate it, reduce it – in a word, destroy it.

The capacity to sacrifice one's life for transcendent values (freedom and justice), a general entity (the homeland, national identity), places us at the heart of morality. After all, it consti-tutes the core of one's experience: when people sacrifice their own lives, die *for*, they think there is something *higher* than mere immanent existence; that there are transcendent standards which go beyond the principle of preservation. The experience and affirmation of this superiority represent the *negation* of what then seems contingent and inessential: our sheerly immanent being, our passively biological existence.

The values, the ideas, we live by are those for which we are prepared to die. And it is as if war, when pitting tyranny against democracy, imperialism against the rights of nations, servitude against freedom, reminds us of the power of these values, which bourgeois comfort, an obsession with material goods, and even (to force the argument) a lasting peace cause us to forget. This is where Hegel does not hesitate to invoke the 'benefit of wars': the reactivation of a sense of what is essential in us. That is precisely why, because it pierces the dialectical structure of patriotic heroism (what makes us live is what causes us to die), he draws lessons from it which, though conceptually 'logical', might seem perfectly monstrous. Thus, there is *nothing like* a war to get us to rediscover fundamental values, the meaning of the difference between the pointless and the essential. For Hegel, a prolonged peace always ends up blunting the edge of ethical experience, clogging up the soul in its egotistical calculations against a backdrop of tranquil prosperity.[8]

To round off this virtuous trinity (self-transcendence, endurance, abnegation), we might cite – something even more ambiguous – an ultimate martial virtue: obedience. Immediate, precise, exhaustive conformity to orders is required of the soldier as a principal virtue. In the army, the soldier is strictly disciplined, and insubordination severely punished. Incorrigible children used to be threatened with being sent off to the Foreign Legion 'to learn obedience'. Obviously, obedience is valuable and indispensable in combat: it makes concerted action possible in pursuit of a shared goal. It represses egotistical instincts and enables self-transcendence. It fosters self-abnegation and a concern for others. But military obedience remains stamped with the seal of an insurmountable ambiguity. On the one hand, it is admirable, demanding, and elevates those who submit to it; on the other, it is automatic and blinkered, corresponding to Voltaire's snapshot describing perfect automata in *Candide*. Military obedience prides itself on being unconditional, unthinking, immune to further discussion, blind.

Forged in the heat of battle, these 'moral forces', from ardour via courage and sacrificial heroism to obedience, were rediscovered when, faced with a reputedly fearsome Russian army in a secretly prepared attack conceived as a blitzkrieg, the Ukrainians confounded the most pessimistic predictions. At the sight of concentrations of massed tanks on the borders, many military specialists announced a 'short' war fatal for Ukraine. As we know, it has been nothing of the sort. These gloomy Western forecasts possibly overestimated the strength of the Russian forces, which were sometimes badly led and often ramshackle. But, above all, our flatly individualistic, atheistic times had forgotten the intensity of these moral forces, which can raise an entire people to the height of their destiny, as if this terrible ordeal harnessed decisive energies.

The moral interpretation of war, the idea that armed conflicts have represented matrices of ethical heroization, is important. As Vauvenargues wrote in his *Réflexions et maximes*, if 'vice foments war' (the reasons for going to war invariably presuppose sordid political calculations on the part of leaders who never directly participate in it), 'virtue does battle in it'. The possibility of a precipitation in battle of moral virtues (courage, abnegation, sacrifice) remains dependent on a few conditions: a certain equality in the exchange of death; respect for the rules of combat; an absence of deceit and dishonesty; the protection of civilian populations and innocents.

Before concluding, I must mention the accursed part of the experience of battle, its black side: the 'dark side of violence'. Tension, fear, stress, adrenalin – these can easily prompt moments of self-oblivion that are at the same time outbursts of rage, the liberation of uncontrollable energy, exasperation, in fury that will give rise to abysmal massacres, mindless killing which does not spare children, women, anyone.[9] We can, of course, spell out the neuro-psychiatric mechanism of these excesses (such as decompensation), the 'reason' for this murderous madness (overcoming one's own fear, avenging dead comrades, and so on); ask how far such excesses serve to conceal the monstrosity of war from participants by drowning in it. We shall return to these 'explanations' later, employing the Freudian notion of the death instinct. There remains the extreme ambiguity of war, capable of revealing, of reawakening in humanity, its highest standards and its most savagely destructive instincts: sublime nobility and atrocious abjection.[10]

3

What Is a 'Just' War?

If, with reference to the quality of the soldier's engagement, a war can be said to be 'moral', can it ever be 'just'? Is it not always declared, decided, started for bad reasons? Is not opting for violence illegitimate in and of itself?

The same indignant declarations are regularly to be heard from virtuous columnists or vigilante editorialists: 'violence in any form is inexcusable'; 'all violence is to be condemned'. In particular, this litany is heard on the occasion of rowdy demonstrations, which sometimes get out of hand on account of small groups intent on destruction, police manoeuvres causing panic, or the anger provoked by an accumulation of frustrations. Absolute intolerance for 'any form' of violence in the media is expected, obligatory, systematic, to the point where it becomes difficult to 'explain', to 'discover the rationale' for violent acts, for one is then immediately suspected of seeking to excuse them, to justify them. To the point also that it becomes impossible to publicly envisage the philosophically grounded possibility of an *intransitive* violence, the question of whose justice cannot be posed because it is merely the expression of an impotent rage. In our time, this intolerance is combined with the creation in the arts of an imaginary saturated with fascinating, unbearable violence, but also with the unlimited extension in public debate of the range of who might 'commit violence', create trauma, compel compassion. The rejection of violence in the real world, combined with its hyper-valorization in the imaginary and accompanied by the unlimited generalization of trauma, manifestly form a *system*.

On this basis, given that every war unavoidably involves suffering and death, psychological violence and physical destruction, the very idea of 'just' war might seem misplaced, shocking, monstrous. Yet no-one would dream of questioning the legitimacy of Ukraine's armed self-defence. We therefore need to posit the existence of a difference between good wars and bad wars, just and unjust wars, depending on *who is waging them* and *why*.

The problem of just war has been formulated and reformulated in a long intellectual tradition that runs in the West from the early Church Fathers to international jurists, from Renaissance humanists to the major political thinkers of the twentieth century. The reflection has been intense, and has ended up yielding at least two quite distinct semantic focus-points: on the one hand, the idea of a 'just cause' that is justified on the basis of its motives; on the other, the theme of a formal, structured war, legitimized on the basis of respect for a certain number of rules that the belligerents impose upon themselves at the point of combat.[1] In addition to these two specific, well-documented cultural forms (*jus ad bellum* and *jus in bello*), we can further examine an archaic representation that connects war and law by an obscure link: the great battle viewed as a court of law proclaiming the grand, scandalous and implacable justice of victory.

When people refer to 'just' war, they are spontaneously thinking of the war of 'just cause'. This raises the issue of the good and bad reasons one might have for going to war, and in these doctrines a certain number of criteria are itemized that make it possible to certify 'good' wars. The theoretical edifice of the just war was developed and carried forward by the Church Fathers who, in the course of speculation spread over ten centuries, provided it with a stable architecture. Paradoxically, the scale of their reflection is explained by the power and intensity assumed in Christianity by demands of peace. Some gospel edicts have left their mark, shocking by their intransigence: 'love your enemies', 'if someone slaps you on the right cheek, turn the other cheek'. A rapid reading of these instructions appears to entail a disqualification, a condemnation of any war, *even of a defensive kind*. And yet, the position of the Christian churches has never been an unconditional rejection of any armed conflict, such intransigence soon seeming dangerous, even irresponsible. How is Saint Ambrose to be answered when he assures us that he who does not come to the aid of the victim is as guilty as the aggressor?[2] Yet aiding someone under attack requires going to war with their adversary. And what is to be said to the soldier who wishes to be baptized? That their role prohibits them from acceptance into the Christian religion? Tertullian and Origen had no hesitation saying so. It was against such excesses that Augustine, for example, set about distinguishing between private violence and public war, maintaining that Christ only ever condemned the former.

In fact, while it identifies with the affirmation of universal love, seeming to imply a rejection of *any* violence, even defensive in kind, the Christian church ended up authorizing wars by fixing very strict conditions for them.

A war can already be Christian to the extent that it is never the subject of eulogy or poetic exaltation. The pagan glory bound up with battles, the cult of war heroes, were ferociously denounced. Here we have a wholly negative first condition: war may only be waged when compelled, without a joyful heart, never motivated by self-interest, but only because the situation demands it.[3]

A second condition, deduced from the distinction between private vengeance and public war, is the initiative of a sovereign authority. This is a necessary, albeit formal, condition: a war is just when it is decided upon and waged by a state, a public authority or a prince.

Thirdly, only an actual injustice can justify initiating a war: *unica et sola causa justa: injuria*. The primary injustice, obviously, is to find oneself under attack, the object of aggression, when one is completely innocent (*innocens*: not harmful), wholly within one's rights. This is a flagrant denial of justice. Self-defence, defence of one's integrity, provides incontrovertible grounds for war. This imbalance, this asymmetry between an invaded country and an invading one, rallied European countries to the Ukrainian cause, making it possible to contrast unjust war with legitimate war. Defensive war is always inherently just. Force is repelled by force. When it is a reaction to an initial aggression, any war is in and of itself legitimate.

Here, we might also remember that Vladimir Putin initially attempted to announce Russian aggression as a *response* to a series of provocations: NATO's violation of an implicit agreement not to expand eastwards; cultural genocide perpetrated against Russians in the Donbas; the presence of Nazi groups, and so on. Even the most cynical of wars is always decked out in defensive rationales.

Following the reactive level, there is a second register of the 'just cause': the reparation of an injustice other than direct aggression. For example, an external power can wage occasional raiding operations outside its borders, pillaging, burning, destroying. Or it can decide on the summary execution of a number of nationals of a neighbouring state. In the long history of humanity and its wars, we come across a myriad different examples of 'injustices' that have served as occasions, levers, and sometimes pretexts for declaring war.

In just war doctrine, the description of war as 'redresser of injustices' takes its bearings from civil law (remedy for a tort) and criminal law (punishment of a crime). The more murderous the just war, and the more suffering it entails (one thinks of the eternal 'collateral damage'), the more it will tend to draw on punitive terminology: it will punish 'rogue states', strike 'murderous tyrants', damage 'oppressive despots', defeat crime lords, and so on. It is as if the ordeals suffered by all were tolerable, acceptable, when what is involved is fighting the representatives of *evil*. Ideally, the just war therefore counterposes the good to the evil, the just to the criminal. It is based on a moral asymmetry between the belligerents.

However, just war theorists add an element to this presentation which, while subtle, is no less crucial: what is called the criterion of 'right intention' (*intentio recta*).[4] This specifically involves differentiating between the 'cause' of the war and a mere pretext. A war is not just if the harm suffered is merely an opportunity for the prince, heedless of backing his opponent into a corner, to start a conflict that will enable him to pursue his own interests, above and beyond what he has suffered. Consideration of injustice must be overriding.

Such is the hard core of the Christian doctrine of just war. Over the centuries, it has undergone at least two extensions that proceed in opposite directions: expansion and restriction.

In criminal law, considerations superior to those of pure expiation inform the meaning of punishment. The author of a crime is punished in order to make them *pay for* it, but also to ensure public security by discouraging future crimes. In the same way, by means of war a state intends to pursue something other than pure *recuperatio*: the achievement of its security *for the future*. For example, Francisco de Vitoria, one of the principal theologians of just war, suggested that one can seek more than simple redress in war: 'a prince may do everything in a just war to secure peace and security from attack'.[5]

Here, we can clearly see that the system of justification wavers a little, and that the calculation is uncertain because *future* harms – which, by definition, are contingent – are taken into consideration. This appraisal of future security, of a

guarantee of the conditions for lasting peace, will lead belligerents to go beyond the logic of strict redress of a grievance. Land
will be seized to consolidate borders; the enemy country will be
bled white to ensure its weakness, and so on. The risk is readily
intelligible: the quest for security can become an end in itself,
and no longer be burdened with justifications in terms of harms
actually suffered. By this logic, we can even anticipate trouble.
Take the concept of 'pre-emptive' war (advanced by the United
States to justify the invasion of Iraq in 2003). It is supposed to
respond to duly documented threats, which, in the event, might
be exaggerated or even imagined, like the presence of weapons
of mass destruction in the case of Iraq. War is thus a way of
responding, but *in advance*, to an attack whose imminence is
envisaged as absolutely certain. Yet the perception of this imminence always remains highly subjective.

In the direction this time of restriction, some theologians add
conditions that end up resembling an attempt to discourage any
desire to go to war. Firstly, a calculation of proportionality: the
harms caused by the 'recovery' of damages must not be greater
than the wrong itself. No matter how much one has been
wronged, the reparation must not be disproportionately costly
– in terms of the dead, the wounded, the destruction visited on
oneself or others. On pain of rendering one's own war unjust
even if the initial motive was good, it is therefore necessary to
adjust the hostile response to the magnitude of what has been
suffered in the way of loss. Further criteria can be cited, such as
that of ultimate resort: having exhausted all other solutions
before deciding to go to war. Finally, some theologians stress

that it is essential to be certain of victory. Even if a state has suffered a wrong, it can only avenge itself if it is absolutely sure it can prevail – so as not to risk provoking unnecessary suffering (but how to be sure?).[6] A final, decisive point under discussion is whether a state can punish injustices committed *elsewhere*, which it does not directly suffer. Whether, for example, as Grotius forcefully asserts, it can go to the aid of a tyrannized people, oppressed populations, and (as Vitoria puts it) invoke 'the authority of the world' (*auctoritas orbi*) to declare war on a state that is guilty of abuses against others.[7]

All of this just war doctrine, elaborated over centuries by Christian theologians, was to be adopted in many of its basic intuitions by modern international law (necessity of a 'just cause', principle of proportionality, and so on). That said, it has little to say about the conduct to be followed *during combat* (what is called *jus in bello*), its preoccupation being the motive for going to war (*jus ad bellum*). We must therefore refer to a second theoretical edifice, devoted this time to the limits that belligerents impose on themselves in the use of their armed forces against enemies once hostilities have begun and armies been deployed on the battlefield.

Killing, agreed: but *not just anyone, not just at any time, not just anyhow*. Appraisal and codification of the rules of the right to kill in war have been elaborated over the last two centuries, to the point of their inscription, recognized by numerous countries, in the Geneva Conventions. Nations have agreed to enshrine a certain number of fundamental prohibitions: respect for civilian populations, for enemy combatants once disarmed, for prisoners of war, for diplomatic personnel; respect also for truces that have been multilaterally decided. We might also refer to two further rules, on the two outer edges of war: the need for a declaration of war coupled with an ultimatum; and the signing of a peace treaty accompanied by an amnesty clause.

The construction of this new doctrine corresponded to a new map of the world. I refer to the 'Westphalian turning point' in the Western world.[8] The old, premodern political space, while still haunted by the restoration of a mystical empire, was splintered into a jumble of principalities with complicated dynastic relationships, fragmented empires and complex federations. This confused space was disappearing in favour of a smoother juxtaposition of sovereign states exercising jurisdiction over a defined territory.

The doctrine of wars of 'just cause' assumed the personalization of power: it was to an individual (the prince) that the question of the morality of his motives, the purity of his 'intention', was posed. But once people started speaking of 'states', the referent became abstract entities whose sovereignty was recognized and, consequently, formed the basis of perfect equality. Whatever its size, religion, natural wealth or population, a state deemed sovereign is formally 'equal' to any other state. The primordial legal effect of this sovereignty (recognition of its equality by other states) has to be the renunciation of the moralism or psychologism that guided the original theories of just war (Is it good or bad? What is its *true* intention?).

Firstly, in effect, war, aggression, against a third party becomes a state prerogative. It does not have to justify itself: that is its right. In declaring war, it is simply exercising it. Before what court should it have to justify itself, given that it is specifically declared to be sovereign? Just wars would continue to be regulated, but in a novel, wholly formal sense, as in the expression 'valid wedding', which signifies a marriage conducted in full conformity with the rules and rites, and which, as a result, has legal effect – in the same sense as one speaks of a 'valid will'. A war is just on the condition that it observes a certain number of specific protocols (prior declaration, respect for diplomatic forms, and so on), without its 'reasons' or other motives ever being at issue. It then becomes 'solemn and public'.[9] The legal effect will be full recognition of the future gains of the war as long as everything has been done within the rules.

This external respect is easy to share, and creates a community between major civilized states. Such mutuality even makes possible the formulation in the doctrine of a concept that might at first sight appear aberrant: war that is 'just on both sides'.[10] It can be just on both sides in as much as each belligerent proves meticulous and scrupulous in observing certain principles, as one would say of two completely fair-playing partners. We can clearly see that we are dealing here with an amoral sense of justice: purely external respect for a certain number of rules.

Secondly, if each state is declared sovereign, states become perfectly equal between themselves *in law*, whatever their real differences. The Christian idea of a war 'of just cause' introduces a (moral) inequality between the belligerents: the good and the bad, the just avenger and the criminal, and so on. This radical inferiorization, this flagrant asymmetry, soon seemed like an insult to the very idea of state sovereignty.

The idea of a war that is 'just on both sides' (reference is also made to war 'in due form') is both appealing and grating. The notion that a state can wage a war it declares 'just' simply because it respects certain protocols, without ever having to declare its motives, might cause indignation given that this decision will entail suffering and death. This amoral conception, which is supposed to protect the principle of state sovereignty, remained acceptable when technologies of destruction (long-range weapons, missiles, nuclear arms, and so on) had not reached the stage that turns wars into atrocious massacres, killing soldiers and civilians indiscriminately – even if it must be acknowledged that old-style battles could be accompanied by raids, plundering, and so on. Our sensitivity to war has been profoundly transformed by two successive world wars that have filled people with horror and their history with atrocities. It has become synonymous with intolerable barbarism. It entails too much indiscriminate, terrible violence for the question of its legitimacy not to be raised. The major post-war international organizations (the League of Nations and then the United Nations) were explicitly established with the aim of preventing new wars, of constructing mechanisms that could compel states to settle their disputes by means other than conflict, to make war no longer their incontrovertible prerogative.

But cannot war that is 'just on both sides' be defended precisely by counting on its limiting effects? For respect for a certain number of rules during combat (sparing civilian populations, not killing an unarmed enemy, treating prisoners well, observing truces) necessarily entails a reduction in suffering and death. We might even go further and find that 'solemn and public' war, refusing to consider conflict from a moral stand-point and making do with instituting respect for the rules of combat, is more humane and less murderous than the 'just cause' war. Indeed, undue moralization of conflicts and radical criminalization of the enemy can render wars more aggressive, more murderous, more 'total'. As soon as one posits a moral contrast between the camp of good and that of evil, the forces of the just and of the unjust, the only possible conditions for peace are the total capitulation and complete destruction of the enemy. Morality introduces an absolutist dimension that can translate into greater brutality and a quest for annihilation on the battle-field. In the past, people fought until the enemy displayed signs of surrendering (a white flag, and so on), the immediate effect of which was to put an end to hostilities: that was the rule.

Should I confront a representative of absolute evil, my duty will be to pursue their total extinction, to annihilate them, not to give them any chance. By contrast, in the case of a war 'just on both sides', the adversary will be declared *justus hostis*: a just enemy. My relationship to them will therefore no longer be moral, but entirely juridical. I will regard them as an equal in the sense that the declaration of war will have given me authorization to kill them under certain conditions. This is why war 'in due form' can induce a certain respect between enemies – or at least not entail hatred. To be at war is to come temporarily under a different regime of law, in which the enemy will be defined as someone whom, while respecting rules, I can kill on the field of battle.

In pitting the just against the unjust, the war of 'just cause' obviously cancels this equality. Hence Kant's warning: 'No war of independent States against each other, can rightly be a war of Punishment (*bellum punitivum*). For punishment is only in place under the relationship of a Superior (*imperantis*) to a Subject (*subditum*); and this is not the relation of the States to one another.'[11] Peace can thus no longer be pursued as the result of a dialectic between military manoeuvres and diplomatic negotiations, each victory on the ground representing nothing more than the possibility of gaining advantage when it comes to the final talks. Does one negotiate with the devil? Does one compromise with evil? If only in the fighting itself, demonization of the enemy undermines *jus in bello* (the laws of battle). Is it not my grave responsibility to be prepared to employ any means, from the most atrociously lethal weapons to the most duplicitous subterfuge, to triumph over evil?

The war of 'just cause' requires that a sovereign power's entry into a state of war exclude any cynical pursuit of self-interest or any futile quest for glory. However, the introduction of a moral asymmetry, by casting war as a struggle between good and evil, could implicitly authorize unlimited violence against the representatives of barbarism, dictating their absolute destruction. For its part, war that is 'just on both sides' assigns each state a right to war as an absolute prerogative, the state being unaccountable to anyone over its decision to go to war and enjoying a scandalous impunity in principle when it decides to seize a neighbour's territory by violence. On the other hand, once war is declared, each belligerent is caught up in a binding juridical configuration that might make it possible to limit suffering by imposing a 'law of war'. Finally, the peace treaty makes it possible to return to pre-war normality by dispelling animosity.

I have outlined in their irreducibility two semantic focal points, each of which involves a determinate sense of justice: either an absolute moral value or an external legality to be respected. Each of the two models has its relevance and its monstrosity. The juridical model hypocritically suspends any moral judgement and refuses to distinguish between aggressors and victims. But it sets limits to itself that are recognized by the two belligerents in their use of violence. The moral model is certainly easier on the conscience, but it seems to justify greater extremism in combat.

With regard to the international law of war, the ideal scenario is obviously the coupling of the two models (*jus ad bellum* and *jus in bello*): wars started for 'just causes' but which have self-imposed limits when it comes to fighting.

To conclude, we can evoke a third form of 'just' war – one that is more obscure and archaic: war that founds law; war that *determines* justice in proclaiming victory. This representation might seem appalling, given that we identify war with the unleashing of violence and the chaos of contending forces, while law should exclusively be the external constraint that prohibits or at least limits them. But the idea that war declares what is right is ancient, and might even be part of humanity's oldest intuitions. It is based both on a myth (the original seizure of land) and a metaphor (battle as a court of law).

The myth is that of the origin of the state. We are familiar with the abstract philosophical version: the social contract. Hobbes, Locke and Rousseau theorized, formalized and analysed the idea of an original pact whereby men unanimously decided to establish a sovereign authority. But beneath these intellectual constructs, there runs an older narrative, which refers any foundation of a state to an initial *coup de force*, a victory in blood that fixes borders and authorizes domination over a whole people:

> War obviously presided over the birth of states; right, peace, and laws were born in the blood and mud of battles . . . the law is born of real battles, victories, massacres, and conquests which can be dated and which have their horrific heroes; the law was born in burning towns and ravaged fields. It was born together with the famous innocents who died at break of day.[12]

Public right is therefore always that which has been wrested from another people – a right, won in blood, that is imposed. While philosophers conceptualize the rational foundation of states against a backdrop of consensual unanimity, mythological grand narratives rediscover the buried, concealed chapters narrating the great violence that presided over the birth of states. They recount how it was always bloodstained victory that created justice – a 'justice' whose sole function was to guarantee one people's domination over another.

If these representations are so horrifying for philosophy, it is because they presuppose a seamless continuity between law and violence, justice and force – a continuity that philosophy has always prided itself on deconstructing. For example, in a chapter of *The Social Contract* (I, 3) Rousseau establishes the absurdity of

the expression 'right of the strongest'. We can immediately sense
how scandalous it seems to envisage the most brutal or the wealth-
iest invoking a 'right' to refer to the violent imposition of their
diktats. But whatever the theoretical reticence, war has long
claimed to say what is right through the clash of arms.

Georges Duby has shown that what the Middle Ages called a
'great battle' is irreducible to the occasional skirmishes punctuat-
ing the tumultuous relations between rival lordships.[13] 'Battle'
was something other than indecisive, recurrent, occasional
clashes. It answered to a principle of concentration. It brought
together, crystallized, a heap of dispersed minor conflicts; the
settling of old scores; punitive, indecisive expeditions. It involved
fighting *once and for all*, concentrating all one's forces to obtain by
arms a definitive *decision* entailing irreversible results. This decision by arms, establishing the right of the dominant over the
vanquished, was ultimately declared dependent on the gods and
subject to their judgement: it was they who, by promoting victory,
made a choice. To be victorious was to see oneself given prefer-
ence by God. Success in war was a consecration of justice that
created a divide, a clean break between victor and vanquished, as
clear-cut as the separation of night from day, good from evil,
black from white. The fact of having agreed to concentrate forces
for this solemn, unique moment (the great battle) divided time,
introducing a caesura between a before and an after.

So, war is just like a court of law. Do trials pertain to combat,
or is it combat that resembles a trial? Each sequence feeds the
other with its images: concentration, decision, binary divide,
irreversibility, and so on. That is how war can be just in this

archaic and atrocious sense, this monstrous tautology: the victor is deemed just simply by virtue of his having been victorious. It is God as supreme judge who, in granting success, indicates on whose side justice and the good are to be found. And woe to the vanquished.

Hegel reverts to this intuition when he makes human history a tribunal, adopting Schiller's verse: 'World history is the tribunal of the world' (*Die Weltgeschichte ist das Weltgericht*).[14] Justice and reason, he thought, are not ideal, transcendent norms, but *processes* that are realized, and that unfold slowly, painfully, but inevitably in, by and through human history: that is, amid and by means of wars, tears and suffering. On the same speculative bases, Marxism would construct the myth of the proletariat's ultimate victory over the bourgeoisie, the dramatic moment of the 'last fight' projected into a glorious future, ensuring the definitive triumph of justice in history.

The myth of history as dispenser of justice scarcely survived two centuries. But the temptation remains to render wars acceptable by framing them as Armageddon, to mythologize them by locating them in the *longue durée*, so that they assume the shape of a final battle supported by eternal gods. The history of humanity remains haunted by wars that claim, in an unprecedented explosion of violence, *to put an end* to war once and for all, ushering in a lasting peace.

So, there are three determinations of what is right: moral, formal, and eschatological. If we take the example of the war in Ukraine, with good reason it is presented in public debate as counterposing an invading aggressor (Russia, as led with an iron grip by Vladimir Putin) to a people under attack defending its right to self-determination and the values of liberty. However, the risk in this ultra-moralization of the war is that, by dint of making the master of the Kremlin the devil incarnate, the end of the war can only be conceived in the form of a capitulation, a surrender, encouraging a military maximalism that might result in general disaster.

Instead, is it not reasonable to think that 'one day' it will be necessary to sit at the negotiating table, and hence, for the duration of a peace settlement and a signature, preserve the fiction of equality between the belligerents? Kant wrote that 'it must still remain possible, even in wartime, to have some sort of trust in the attitude of the enemy, otherwise peace could not be concluded'.[15] This is the caution Emmanuel Macron seemed to have in mind when he uttered his 'Putin must not be humiliated', which, at the time, seemed excruciatingly discordant and scandalous, given it coincided with an evocation of the war crimes committed by the Russian army.

In any event, that is precisely the problem: Have the conditions of the 'trust' invoked by Kant survived between Russians and Ukrainians following Mariupol and Bucha? Or must we say that we shall have to make these terrible deaths the inevitable 'profit and loss' of any war, *forget* them so as to be able to restore the fiction of equality between two sovereign states at the moment a peace agreement is signed? Is it even possible to do otherwise, unless the primary goal is the destitution of Vladimir Putin himself? But do we know what will happen *afterwards*?[16]

4

The State Makes War and War Makes the State

A key teaching of just war theory is that only a *sovereign* authority can decide on a war – something that Rousseau would reformulate, stating, 'War is . . . not a relationship between one man and another, but a relationship between one State and another.'[1] This relationship between states is not simply one of origin or initiative. While it is clearly the state which makes war, it remains to be examined whether it is not equally the case that *war makes the state*. It perhaps derives its depth, its continuing existence, from a permanent 'state of war'. If so, that would be its 'element', as is the sea for sharks: the state cannot survive without it.

We must reflect on this intertwinement. To do so, we can begin by setting out three images (at once representation and metaphor) of the state – as a collective body or living organism; as an artificial social unit, a fragile collection of individuals soldered together by a 'social pact'; as an image projected by a power, a colourful story, a national legend – and then show, in each instance, how the state's need for war is deducible from it.

By 'state' is to be understood not simply an administration, an institution sustained by its officials, a centre of public decision-making. The state is also a country defined by borders, a people unified by common laws, culture, and sometimes language. From very early on – antiquity at least (Plato, Cicero, and so on) – this compact assemblage, this dense unit, has been compared to the living body of a human or animal.[2] The metaphor leads to a whole series of theses and conceptual propositions. First of all, there is the idea that, if the state is like an animal, it requires 'living space' in order to thrive and grow. If the space circumscribed by current borders seems too restricted and suffocating, then war will be the natural instrument for *expansion*, enabling a nation to reach its optimum size.

It will be said that this is crude social Darwinism (life as the selection of the fittest, the strongest through struggle), or perverted Nietzscheanism (life as the will-to-power finding joy and fervour in domination).[3] In any event, this initial synthesis assumes that the state has vital requirements that war alone is capable of satisfying: conquering new territories; testing and guaranteeing the domination of the strongest; appropriating natural resources or cultural heritages in order to provide the home population with opportunities for renewed vitality, expansion, self-expression; ensuring supremacy over allegedly inferior people who can be reduced to slavery. Needless to say, this series of statements has had a sinister ring since Hitler combined them in *Mein Kampf*.

One way of escaping unduly 'Darwinian' representations of life, giving it a less biological cast, would be to think about it instead as existence polarized by values, projects and narratives. In the broader sense of existence, life senses its unity, discovers its identity, and experiences its authenticity precisely when they are threatened in their integrity and values by an *enemy*. The enemy is what challenges them, representing a serious danger, but by that very token determines them. It is now a question of saying the enemy reveals to me *what I really am*, makes me understand what defines me. In and through the vital surge the enemy provokes is revealed what counts above all else for me and what I am ready to die for. The enemy discloses to life its profundity. To articulate this intuition, Carl Schmitt rediscovered and commented on a verse by German poet Theodor Däubler, 'The enemy is our own question as form': 'The enemy is not something that must be suppressed for one reason or another and destroyed because he is lacking in value. The enemy is on a par with me. For this reason, I must come into conflict with him to acquire my own measure, my own limits and my own form.'[4]

This surge is perhaps what Europe is experiencing with the war in Ukraine. We might almost say that Europe is being constituted *for the first time*, with irreducible intensity, as a *properly political* community by discovering an enemy. It recognizes itself as the bearer of certain values and the defender of a particular way of life, committed to freedom of expression, when the question is posed: Over and above political or economic calculations, am I prepared to recognize in Vladimir Putin's Russia an enemy and in Volodymyr Zelensky's Ukraine a friend? To illustrate the point, we might adopt Carl Schmitt's disturbing formulation: 'The specific political distinction to which political actions and motives can be reduced is that between friend and enemy.'[5]

The vitalist dimension of wars can therefore be expounded in two ways. In its biological version, it regards war as the expression of a vital, aggressive and brutish instinct of peoples (in search of space, quick to dominate the weakest, and so on). In its more existential version, it regards war as the surge that endows life with its profundity and reveals to it its true identity.

But much of political modernity has consisted in outright rejection of a perspective that inscribes the state in some primal naturalness. The 'contractualist' schema has been preferred. Therein the state is a fragile, artificial organization, born of an *understanding* between men and expressing a desire to live together. Here, it is Hobbes's oeuvre that shows how this presentation of a state arising from an initial agreement explains and entails the necessity of war. In Hobbes's *De Cive* or *Leviathan*, we find the founding thesis of our political modernity: the state is an artificial body arising from the volition of men, arising from the unanimous relinquishment of their natural rights, the consequence of a pact between them to 'make society' and accept common obedience under a unique recognized authority.

But if individuals have contracted together, it is done to escape the worst possible fate: anarchy, continual mutual destruction, the 'war of all against all'. This is the first level of meaning of war, described by Hobbes in Chapter 13 of *Leviathan*. It refers to a chronic state of poverty, distress, instability and inter-individual violence, until the state finally imposes inviolable rules of cohabitation. Without an overarching iron will that governs them all, men inexorably imbibe the poison of their fratricidal struggles. The point is therefore to create a state of social stability, public tranquillity, *civil peace*, by compelling all subjects into a common obedience to public laws. The birth of the state is what makes it possible to escape the original war of all against all.

But there are many states, each of which can be thought threatening by another, given (or supposedly given – the rather thin mercantilist version adopted by Fichte, for example) that it can only grow by diminishing an adversary, enriching itself by impoverishing its neighbour.[6] There are *numerous* states, and, as long as they do not sense an authority above them drastically regulating their relations, they will eternally find themselves in a 'state of war' (this is the second level of meaning), as were men formerly – not in the precise meaning that this expression assumes when it comes to describing continual interindividual violence in the state of nature ('war of all against all'), but in the sense of a constant structural possibility of interstate hostilities: war as *real potentiality*. It is like bad weather, Hobbes says: it does not signify incessant torrents, but the possibility that it will rain at any moment.[7]

At a third level of meaning, we shall find the dated historical sense of war as a determinate conflict between particular political units (with start and end dates, decisive battles) and peace as a likewise clearly dated period free of such conflict (ratified by treaties and alliances, and then shattered by some provocation).

Finally, at a fourth level, outlined on the horizon of time as luminous, utopian post-history, is the dream of a permanent state of peace between human beings.

The idea of the 'social contract' thus unfolds *three* levels of meaning: the *myth* of an original war between individuals; the *structural possibility*, untranscendable between states, of a conflict lasting throughout their history; and finally, *real*, actual, periodized wars. A corresponding tripartite division applies to peace: the public within a territory ruled by a sovereign who protects it; a state of suspended, temporary non-war between two or more states; the millenarian reverie of a plenitude of tranquillity and order at the end of history.

This complex edifice discloses six cells of meaning. To understand what thinking about war involves, we need to relate them to one another. For example, the 'first' war – that of the origins ('war of all against all') – pertains to fable rather than established historical fact. Yet its political impact is powerful. If a strong state, common laws and impeccable police are required, it is because there is a permanent threat of reversion to the initial state of anarchy.

At the same time, it might be asked why it is assumed that man is the natural enemy of man. Who convinced us that, absent the state, men would be condemned to tear each other apart? To undermine such verities, we could cite the demystifying cry of

Léo Ferré in his anarchist manifesto, *Il n'y a plus rien*: 'Disorder is order minus power!' Was not the fable of initial anarchy invented *precisely* in order to make us obey? In fact, we know nothing about the condition of men in the state of nature. In his *Discourse on Inequality*, Rousseau, for example, challenged the thesis of the original war of all against all from which we were supposedly rescued by state invention. What if primitive man was a peaceful fellow, and what if violence was the bitter fruit of 'living in society'?

Except that, if we refer to Hobbes, the inanity of Rousseau's fable becomes clear; all it takes is a brief look at how states behave with each other – at the incessant, terrible wars waged by those who (once again) have no sovereign authority above them to restrain their violence. External war is how internal obedience is obtained. Because it attests to the blood-soaked way in which things transpire between states, it imparts *substance* to the phantom of primitive civil war between individuals; it dramatizes it: this is how things might turn out *between you* if you do not obey.[8]

Another way of defending the idea that waging war on the Other makes it possible to strengthen the cohesion of the Same would be to show how the image of the *enemy* has the capacity to unify an entire people. Countless thinkers have denounced this atrocious instrumentalization of war by the state – conjuring up an enemy to artificially create the unanimity that would otherwise be lacking.

There are several ways of construing the fabrication of unity in and through war. The first is to deplore the presence in any society of disruptive elements (dissolute youth, incorrigible troublemakers) who fracture social harmony. You just have to channel their unbridled energy by sending them off to war! War, wrote Jean Bodin, is a formidable 'cleanser' of such 'impure' elements (which he went so far as to characterize as 'swine').[9] It cleanses the republic's body of disruptive agents, enabling it to recover a healthy constitution by expelling to turbulent borders those with overexcited temperaments for whom battle is a way of discharging their aggression and releasing their brute energy.

But we can think of other, more serious roots of division in a republic than the presence of 'hotheads': the inequalities in living standards that feed jealousy; the hierarchies that lead to social humiliation; the displays of wealth that fuel frustration – and much else. Hence a second set of statements: brandishing the spectre of a public enemy, war diverts negative energies from their primary object, creates consensus by directing them against another, and finally makes people forget their disagreements by focusing their attentions on a shared hatred. We have many reasons to envy one another, to tear one another apart, but we detest the external enemy even more. In the *Discourses*, Machiavelli was to say that internal peace is secured through external warfare: it solders together the political community.[10]

In an astonishing, provocative text, Erasmus reveals the supreme depravity, the best-kept secret: states that secretly come to an agreement once they sense that their subjects might direct their anger at their leaders:

what is the basest and most flagitious conduct of all, there are crowned heads, who, with the mean cunning that ever characterizes the despot, contrive (because they find their own power weakened by the people's union, and strengthened by their division), to excite war without any substantial reason for a rupture; merely to break the national union at home, and pillage the oppressed people with impunity.[11]

War is a good way to unify, but this union is constructed around a central division between dominant and dominated, rulers and ruled, which is never examined, and invariably concealed by the blinding light of external conflicts.

We have hitherto considered war in relation to the state's need for order, cohesion, obedience and unity. But the texture of the state is also determined by its relationship with other political entities. It is threatened not only with internal laceration and implosion, but also with encroachment, rapine and invasion from without. Take the European space: throughout its modern and contemporary history, it has been shot through with incessant wars, and the Ukrainian conflict indicates that the twenty-first century will, alas, be no exception. As regards Europe, we recall once more the break represented by the Treaty of Westphalia (1648). The premodern European political space comprised overlapping lordships, complex royalties, riven by interminable dynastic rivalries, and above all haunted by the mystical dream known as the 'kingdom of the last days'. Fostered by various oracular sources, the idea was that the sign of Christ's imminent return would be the advent of an empire with no borders, one as smooth, unified, and continuous as Christ's seamless cloak. The dream of a universal monarchy would be pursued until at least Charles V. Until the end of the Renaissance, any significant war was imperial in inspiration, whether waged by Spain, France or Germany, each of which in turn designated itself the epicentre of a mystical empire.

The Treaty of Westphalia introduced a new, secularized meaning to war, revolving around the state's immanent interests rather than its transcendent vocation. Henceforth, the European space was to be regarded as composed of a multiplicity of juxtaposed nation-states whose respective powers were made to 'balance one another'. But this equilibrium was dynamic and fragile, always to be restored, corrected, amended. Wars were murderous games to re-establish balance: they were explained and justified as so many attempts on the part of one power to weaken another that threatened to become preponderant, to break up an alliance between minor states that would form too sizeable an entity. These calculations, and the reconfigurations brought about by the contingencies of economic or political circumstances, required that, every decade at least, war broke out to correct the European 'balance' created by the respective weight of nations. Once again, the state discovers in war the wherewithal to ensure its rank, guarantee its preservation, defend its vital interests, and ultimately find salvation.

☙

One last lesson on the tie that binds the state to war, each being the *condition* of the other, must stress the imaginary dimension. There is no doubting the existence of flesh-and-blood rulers and ministers, solidly built parliaments and palaces, and physically demarcated borders defining a national territory. But all these real personnel and devices are supposed to embody, represent and defend a 'state' as image, abstraction – a rather fluid proper noun. The state is the 'ideality' that constructs its reality in people's heads. In the first instance, it is a *reputation*, the image of a power projecting itself in people's imaginary. During the Peloponnesian War – the fratricidal rivalry between Athens and Sparta – Thucydides was the first to explore this imaginary dimension, as well as the necessity of war implied by it, in a tremendous dialogue invented by him that fascinated Leo Strauss.[12] I shall provide a bare-bones summary of the conversation, invented by the Greek historian, between representatives of Athens and Melos. The context is as follows: Melos, a small island at the centre of the Aegean Sea, was intent on remaining neutral, and refused to enter into the Athenian empire's sphere of influence. The latter had no real *need* to annex this island, which did not represent a genuine threat. The whole dialogue revolves around a different order of necessities, at once more subtle and more compelling. Athens argues as follows: in refusing to submit, in stating a desire to remain neutral, you are doing us a great wrong. The independence you seek to display sets a terrible example. Reflect a little: we have the ability to impose our power on you; we have the capacity to dominate you. If we do not do so, what will people say? That we are magnanimous, respectful of other people's freedom? No, obviously, everyone will say the opposite: this Athens that people thought so impressive, well, it seems to be diminishing, declining, faltering. A small island lies within range of its power and it does not swallow it up? For, as we know, the difference between physical power and political power consists in this: physical force exists in and through its manifestations, whereas what is called 'power' essentially belongs to those who have *the reputation of possessing it*. It consists in this *supposed* capacity for influence. And that reputation must be nurtured by victories.

The geopolitical imperative is the reverse of the moral imperative. Kant expressed it clearly: you can because you must. The moral law compels me to act. For his part, Thucydides proposes: you must because you can. Such are the overriding constraints of the image: the image of my power obliges me to dominate what I can dominate so as to build my reputation. The problem is that the 'state' is neither a big beast moved by predatory instincts, nor a fragile agreement between individuals, but a spectral being, a fable in people's heads that is to be maintained by war.

Rousseau understood this when he envisaged writing some 'principles for war': the real constraint on a state – at bottom, an essentially composite, uncertain being – is *to feel it exists*. To that end, as Demosthenes had already said in connection with Athens, there are funeral orations.[13] And, logically, because they precede them, there are wars. War, in which one is supposed to die 'for', gives the nation a unique vibrancy: it defends itself, it fights, it signs declarations of hostilities, peace treaties, truces, and so on. The state ultimately feels that it scarcely exists in the monotony, the sluggishness of its ordinary administration, the abstraction of its laws. By contrast, in police repression, in military decision-making or appeals to the defence of its integrity, it feels alive!

But it has to live up to its image. While the surprise of the Ukrainian conflict initially lay in the unilateral unleashing of war, it has also consisted in the failure of a blitzkrieg. Kyiv did not fall. The reputation of the Russian army, its assumed shock power, its putative massiveness have not been enough to extinguish the taste for freedom among women and men determined to live differently.

The conclusion is in Machiavelli's favour. No-one has surpassed him when it comes to connecting internal affairs (public order) to external ones (foreign policy) in a common understanding of the state and war. The first proposition is as follows: the ruler's sole, constant preoccupation must be the art of war.[14] As we know, *The Prince*'s break with previous 'philosophical treatises' on the art of governing, from Plato's *Statesman* to Aquinas's *De regno*, consists in the absence from his work of any interrogation of the profound legitimacy, the metaphysical essence, the rational or theological foundation, of the government of men. One question, one obsession, runs through his work: What are the *techniques* for preserving power? The banality of the question conceals the most secret, scandalous statement in *The Prince*: power *is always what I have wrested from the previous leader*; and a pretender is lurking in the shadows hoping to seize it from me. Certainly, the posts *in themselves* are legitimate: a prince is *necessary*, and he *needs* ministers, who in turn require intendants. The roles are always intrinsically worthy, justified. But *who* is to occupy these posts, especially the *first?* It will be given to the most cunning and the strongest, the lion who knows how to play the fox. Between prince and ministers, between minister and intendants, there is perpetual war, each subordinate looking for a sign of weakness in his superior to swoop in and replace him. But this is not a civil war pitting the people against its corrupt rulers or involving two opposing factions within the same population. It is the muffled war between the prince and his closest 'friends'. Hence Machiavelli's fundamental republicanism: a prince's most loyal ally is the *people*, who have but one desire – not to be *overly* ruled.

In the same way, and for the same reasons (complete lack of legitimacy: neither blood nor qualifications – big words that only deceive mobs – are of any help), princes engage in perpetual war among themselves, each of them watching for the slightest sign of despondency or fatigue. For the state, the art of war is its *survival* technique; it is the sign that, for all the founding narratives and other myths of origin, political power *never has roots*. A host of economic reasons can be found for war (we shall return to this). But the most secret and decisive reason, concealed by rhetoric about the justice of the cause, is this: the radical *contingency of power*.[15]

5
The Idea of Total War

When denouncing the atrocities of Russian forces or trying to assess whether NATO risks allowing itself to be dragged into a direct conflict with Russia, journalists discussing the war in Ukraine have often reawakened the spectre of 'total war'. The same expression has been used by the head of Russian diplomacy (Sergei Lavrov) to condemn the West's aggressive responses, ranging from economic sanctions to forms of cancel culture. Variously employed, the concept has a history we can only outline here and carries with it a whole philosophy of violence and its (non-)limits that we need to educe.

The 'official' history of the phrase begins in the 1920s and '30s. At issue, descriptively and normatively, was an understanding of what had happened to Europe during four years of interminable, suicidal conflict, the First World War, and also the nature of the break represented by such colossal collective violence. Two reference points, taken from the two principal belligerents, are Léon Daudet's book *La Guerre totale* (1918) and one by Erich Ludendorff, general-in-chief of the German army, *Der Totale Krieg* (1935).[1] Both sought to think through the lessons of the global conflict, but also the socio-military conditions for victory were such a tragedy to be repeated. If the expression 'total war' took root among military men and intellectuals at this precise point, it would soon become an interpretative grid, a key to retrospective understanding for historians, and a clue to a mystery for philosophers.

The former used it to try to determine a point of rupture or change of direction even before the First World War: the moment when the goal of wars became complete destruction of the enemy rather than mere assertion of superiority. Many stressed the revolutionary wars that inflamed Europe from 1792 onwards in the name of new political ideals and, in their wake, Napoleon's campaigns to reconstruct an empire with a combination of speed and brutality. Some went back much further, recalling Roman injunctions at the time of the Punic Wars: *Delenda est Carthago!* ('Carthage must be destroyed!') Yet others evoked Genghis Khan's lightning construction of the Mongol Empire by raids six centuries later. By definition, total domination of the world is not shared!

But also at issue was the identification of an enigmatic relationship: that between war and violence. It might be thought strange even to raise the question, for, ultimately, war, by definition, is violence. To speak of war is, alas, to presuppose the wounded and the dead, destruction and exile. At the same time, however, it is impossible to accept that war amounts to uncontrollable chaos, the unleashing of unbridled violence. To speak of war is to speak of customs, rules, signs, frameworks, discipline and limits. The problem can be reformulated as a set of questions: Is war what makes it possible to regulate, to control violence? Or is this appearance of regularity a hypocritical principle of acceptability, or even an enormous lie? Hence the problem: If total war means the reign of unlimited violence, must we say that it reveals the profound truth of any war? Or, alternatively, does it represent a betrayal of its essence? This is an unfathomable problem, but one which traces a horizon from which we can fix the meaning of the term by mobilizing three notions: all-out offensive, absolute enemy, and general mobilization.

War can be deemed *total* in the first sense of an absence of any limits to aggression. Here it might immediately be objected: Ultimately, in war, is it not basically a question of killing the greatest number of enemies, destroying positions, neutralizing a hostile army? And is any kind of neutralization more effective than *annihilation*? Yet such verities are abstract. When Renaissance princes employed *condottieri* mercenary armies hired at great cost, they made them function 'economically'. We might also recall the long-drawn-out character of siege wars in the seventeenth century, which above all else required soldiers to put up with cold and boredom. In the age of Enlightenment, combat involving sizeable armies might make do with skirmishes, with a few exchanges of fire, but readily accepted uncertain outcomes. Or you ducked out at the last moment. You could even carry out adroit delaying manoeuvres to unsettle your opponent, without ever giving battle. Reference has been made to *guerres en dentelles* ('wars in lace') to designate conflicts waged by officers with a proliferation of rituals of approach and signs of mutual 'respect', parading on symbolic portions of territory. This did not prevent some pre-revolutionary wars from being horribly murderous, such as the first Italian wars (1494–95), when *la furia francese* was denounced. Or think of the Battle of White Mountain (1620), which marked the end of the Kingdom of Bohemia. But these all-out attacks were not the norm — far from it. The norm is to be sought in a whole series of dynastic, aristocratic, and ritualized conflicts.

The veritable break in the modern West dates back to the wars of 1792. Revolutionary France's campaigns against the monarchies of Europe were already striking for their enthusiasm. The lack of professionalism among those involved was made up for by their ardour; they were unorganized but extremely impetuous, driven by a zealous conviction that they were fighting for the liberation of peoples and against oppression. Guibert, an Enlightenment strategist, sensed the impending profound change when he wrote in 1790:

When nations themselves take part in war, everything will change: the inhabitants of a country becoming soldiers, they will be treated as enemies; fear of having them against you, anxiety about leaving them behind, will cause them to be destroyed. Ah! It was a happy invention this fine art, this wonderful system of modern warfare that only mobilized a certain quantity of forces to resolve the quarrel between nations, and which left all the rest in peace, which substituted discipline for number, weighed success by science and constantly placed ideas of order and preservation at the heart of the cruel necessities entailed by war.[2]

As long as wars arrayed princes or lords against one another, as long as they were intended to resolve dynastic conflicts, to parade symbolically, to preserve an etiquette-conscious caste, they remained limited. The modern war of nations, citizens and ideas would change the world.

New times, new wars, new violence: to the revolutionary conviction of fighting for something other than pay, the Napoleonic armies would add a culture of brutality. Bonaparte scorned shrewd calculations and complex manoeuvres. He trusted exclusively in brute force. To strike, to strike as hard as possible: the only military genius consisted in distributing the blows. Only theoretically did a battle directly counterpose two armies, whose size and firepower were to be considered in general. Given the contingencies of movement, travel time and uneven terrain, in the event it was always one regiment against another. Ultimately, it sufficed to be the stronger locally, at the time and in the place where the clash occurred, not *generally*. Speed was gained by living off the country. Above all, the enemy was to be pursued, decimated when down, and victory completed. The dogma of pursuing the enemy (continuing to bombard them with fire even when they were retreating, rather than simply proclaiming victory) indicates that Napoleon sought capitulation, not surrender. Brutality is the effective employment of force that holds nothing back. But it is also a reputation that terrorizes, the chilling conviction in the opponent's heart that they will be given no quarter. The peculiarity of total war in this first sense is therefore that it no longer merely seeks formal victory, proclaiming superiority when the other retreats, but pursues their total collapse.

If annihilation is the inevitable consequence of an all-out offensive, two rival strategies, pertaining to the same logic of total war, can yield the same effect of dissolution: attrition and dislocation. Attrition consists in wearing down the opponent by forcing them to endure a continual deluge of fire, bombarding them without respite. Here we might think of the way that Russian troops were able to 'conquer' the towns of the Donbas before occupying them militarily (Sievierodonetsk, Mariupol, and so on): by subjecting them to constant rocket and missile fire, eating away at resistance. Dislocation consists in turning movements that seek to cut an army off from its base, to provoke a collapse of its body which, trapped and no longer feeling supported by the rear, panics and implodes. Such was the Ukrainian strategy for reconquering various towns in the east, north and south of the country in September and October 2022.

Stunned by an all-out offensive, exhausted by attrition tactics, or forsaken by manoeuvres of dislocation, the enemy army goes into meltdown. But if, in the context of a total war, annihilation rather than surrender is what is sought, it is also because the enemy is believed not to share the same world as us, to partake of a monstrous otherness that justifies pursuit of their *erasure*, annihilation, complete elimination. Carl Schmitt thus contrasted the 'just enemy' (*justus hostis*) of classical wars to the 'absolute enemy' of total wars.[3] In a war deemed 'good form', 'classical', 'regulated', each camp – especially the senior officers who determine the conduct of the fighting – nurtures the conviction that the opponent belongs to the same world as itself (the military universe), sharing the same code of honour, the same concern for etiquette, the same respect for some basic rules of combat. War resembles a sport or game more than it does an enterprise of extermination. Only then is it possible to tone down any notion of absolute hostility in the idea of the enemy. Instead, reference will be made to a 'conventional' enemy, and 'without hatred'. In this style of war, as Rousseau put it so well, 'individuals are enemies only *by accident*, not as men, nor even as citizens'.[4]

To sustain a total war, one has to persuade oneself that the enemy is the embodiment of a moral abomination which legitimizes the ferocity of the fighting. My opponents do not belong to the same universe as me. They are monsters to be exterminated because their existence threatens the existence of my world and my values. Holy wars are total wars in which, in the name of God and with an extremism commensurate with what is at stake, one does battle with infidels, hardened unbelievers, whose very existence is an insult to the true religion in the eyes of the fanatical. To set about the complete destruction of these enemies 'from without' is thus to glorify one's God. Colonial wars too are total wars where one fights a humanity decreed 'inferior', bestialized. In both instances, one can massacre without any qualms.

In a professedly 'just' war, in the sense of 'just cause', Schmitt argues, there is the risk of an intention to annihilate the other. Because the opponents are demonized, criminalized, treated as a representative of evil, their moral inferiority authorizes their being treated with maximum severity. If the enemy is a monster, there is no monstrosity in any means of killing him. Can we even speak of a 'war crime' when fighting criminals?

The very nature of the enemy (infidel, 'savage', criminal) transforms the war aim. It is no longer limited or 'political' in the narrow sense of the term (territorial expansion, symbolic seizures, dynastic revenge, and so on), but becomes moral and absolute. The war's messianic aim introduces an absolutist dimension that has its counterpart, its echo, in a deregulation of customs: to crush infamy, any method will do. When the goal is political in the messianic sense (abolition of an old world, advent of a just society, transformation of existence, and so on), we find the same extremism in violence. An absolute enemy must be destroyed because it prevents humanity from achieving self-fulfilment, and the world from enjoying a lasting peace. Ideological wars are the worst: no negotiation is possible when opposed worldviews are arrayed against one another.

Paradoxically, the more moral the war aim, the more acceptable it is to abandon morals in prosecuting the war. Taking this to its furthest extension, we can imagine the most deregulated, most atrocious war being one that aspires to create eternal, definitive peace. As long as peace is only ever the interval between two armed conflicts, as long as it is a juridical state, war constitutes the 'reasonable' gap in which, amid the fighting, peace is already being prepared. But if it is a moral absolute, a millenarian promise, the war intent on creating it loses any principle of internal limitation.

Once again, we encounter the equivalent of the aporia already condemned in connection with the two senses of 'just' (or moral or regulated) war: if you absolutize peace, you will deregulate war (to put an end to war, extreme means are legitimate); if you banalize war, you devalue peace (you accept that violent deaths caused in the interests of states are not in themselves a scandal).

The original historical meaning of total war (dating from the 1930s) is far removed from these themes of all-out offensive and absolute enemies. The idea of *mobilization* was dominant. According to this idea, a 'total' conflict is one that compels all of a nation's vital forces to participate in the war effort. The mobilization of men takes place through compulsory conscription: all fit men will be sent to the front – we are dealing with a *levée en masse*. Women are mobilized in multiple roles: replacing peasants on farms and absent workers in factories, taking care of children, keeping up the morale of husbands or relatives at the front, and so on. Material capacity is also mobilized: the priority of industry and agriculture alike supports military operations. And minds themselves are mobilized, their sole concern being to reinforce the soldiers' morale and confidence in victory. The war Vladimir Putin is waging against Ukraine is becoming more total, in this sense, by the day: Russia has introduced a war economy, requisitioning factories (any firm can be compelled to accept a military contract on terms set by the state) and minds (any criticism is ferociously repressed).

The mobilization of resources during the First World War, the systematic draining of wealth, the concentration of investment, the appropriation of brains – these measures impressed and awed in the twofold sense of fright and fascination. Ernst Jünger provided an arresting description of them in his *Total Mobilization* (*Die totale Mobilmachung*, 1935).[5] The essay describes how, after the war of knights and monarchs, came that of workers. War had become a vast furnace consuming men, a machine grinding bodies and steel, squandering enormous quantities of energy. Comprehensive demand with a view to fearful destruction: total war is perhaps nothing other than a metaphor for capitalism, or even its completion, in its colossal excess. It crushes and grinds bodies as one would ore; it produces corpses on an industrial scale.

To grasp the modernity of the concept, we must attend to this technological dimension. The idea of mobilization could mislead us if it is assumed to refer only to the vital dimension. For example, Machiavelli recalls that the most terrible wars occur

> when a whole people with all its families leaves a place, driven thence either by famine or by war, and sets out to look for a new home and a new country in which to live . . . it takes possession of every single thing, and expels or kills the old inhabitants. This is war of the most cruel and terrifying kind.[6]

In life-and-death situations, it is eat or be eaten. This vital register has great intuitive force, but it neglects the core modern
meaning of total war: over and above the radical exigencies of
life, the implacable logic of technology. At the intersection of
the destruction of life and the solicitation of energy, we find the
vertigo and insanity that exceed the very possibilities of biological life, ushering us into the mad furnace of technological
modernity demanding ever more deaths in order to produce
ever more machines of destruction. Beyond the vital register,
the idea of mobilization refers to a 'commissioning' of all that
exists. Everything, indiscriminately, can and must serve: metals,
souls, plants, bodies; no parcel of matter, no breath of existence,
will be neglected. For Hannah Arendt, this brutal, no-holds-
barred provision of brains and assets is at the heart of totalitarian regimes.[7] She detects it in propaganda methods and economic
planning alike. For his part, evoking 'enframing', Heidegger
unveiled the essence of technology in identical terms.[8]

In this sense, capitalism is nothing other than a total war
waged on nature: it requisitions the latter. In a totalitarian
regime, as in capitalist industry, the priority is maximum
productivity, the active regimentation of things and minds:
nothing must be permitted to escape this appropriation. War, it
will be said, adds the element of death to this logic. But is not
exploitation also a logic of destruction?

The dimension of death, which might seem like a simple
summation of wars, actually leads us straight to the accursed
part of modernity. After all, the impression that could take hold
of combatants in what has been described as the 'butchery' of

the First World War, when they went up to the front, rifle in hand, and were mown down in their thousands on the fields of the Somme, was that they were acting as raw material for an industry of mass destruction, a compulsive consumer of bodies and steel. Technological devouring had no limits; the pathetic war aims (pushing the enemy front back by a few kilometres) had become a pretext for keeping the death machine running. Here, war is no longer 'the continuation of politics by different means' (in Clausewitz's formula), but the enrolment of the political by war for its own proliferation, its own amplification.[9] It becomes a machine whose destructive purpose hoovers up everything.

Perhaps this industrial horror even lies behind the temptation to demonize the enemy. Our technologies of destruction become so monstrous that if they do not want to appear monstrous in their own eyes, those employing them are obliged to tell themselves that they are using them against an even more monstrous enemy. To de-demonize technology, it is necessary to demonize the enemy.[10]

6
Why War?

Why do human beings wage war? And why have they done so for so long?

These are dizzying questions, which many disciplines have sought to answer, solemnly unveiling their ultimate explanation. Anthropology, economics, psychology, history, psychoanalysis, political science, philosophy: each theory claims to reveal *the* fundamental cause. But every response, however sophisticated or profound, remains unsatisfactory, as if something was decidedly *resistant*. Violence remains the rock on which thinking always breaks.

I propose here to set out an aetiological trinity to be found with remarkable consistency, century after century, in the great thinkers about war – for example, in the works of Thucydides, Hobbes and Raymond Aron. Obviously, the precise terms change from one text to the next, but the semantic focal points remain the same. There are, it is argued, three reasons for war:

greed, fear, and the pursuit of glory. Three fundamental passions, dubbed 'natural' by Hobbes, three elementary, unavoidable motions of the soul, supposedly lie at the root of all wars.

Before opening out this triptych, and in order to forestall a recurrent kind of explanation claiming to be more incontrovertible than our reference to three major passions, we might entertain the notion that the human species is inclined to war quite simply because a kernel of savagery, of bestial instincts, persists in it, impelling each of its members to go for the jugular of their fellow human beings. When one poses the question 'Why war?' the commonest responses offer the following kind of explanation: despite all the efforts to civilize humanity, it possesses too much bestial aggressiveness and too few civilizational barriers to prevent its reversion to the state of savagery

This kind of explanation – a 'bestiality' always ready to resurface – is too thin, even if it can be encouraged, in the case of the war in Ukraine, by an account of the atrocities of Russian soldiers, who are compared to brutes, barbarians, bloodthirsty wild wolves. In the first instance, this is because it is tautological: if man is bellicose, it is because he is shot through with aggressive instincts. Secondly, this explanatory schema might at a stretch seem relevant in accounting for murderous, insane conduct in the heat of battle. But it glosses over the fact that the *decisions* to start wars or battles are taken in impeccably civilized political circles or military staff committees, fed by calculations as well informed as they are cynical. Above all, it rests on an unexamined presupposition: Is the animal kingdom actually as violent as human wars prove to be? Certainly, interspecies violence exists in the animal world, and among big cats hunting naturally relies on aggressive instincts. But when it comes to the wolf confronting the lamb, and the lion the antelope, is it reasonable to speak of 'war'? You might as well say that humanity, the great carnivore, has declared war on the whole animal kingdom in subjecting it to the law of its stomach!

If it is thought that violence between animals can enlighten us about the wars human beings wage *against each other*, we must turn to intraspecies violence – study, for example, the furious battles between tigers, wolves, and so on. Yet here ethologists give us food for thought.[1] If they acknowledge the existence of innate aggressiveness, it is to register two things: On the one hand, the fact that it is unleashed in pursuit of ends that immediately set limits to it – marking or defending territory, designating a pack leader, possessing females. This violence has a highly 'conservative' aim: to structure the group's cohesion and ensure its continuity. It is never gratuitous, still less lethal. When one of the two felines engaged in a furious battle for predominance puts an end to it, it is by presenting its neck, or the most vulnerable part of its body, to its opponent: a single stroke of the claws and death is certain. This posture suffices to eliminate aggression in the other. We shall not find any cruel relentlessness, any gratuitous ferocity, in these animal battles. In fact, man alone is truly *bestial*; animals never are – with the exception of those that have been domesticated . . . Sadistic cruelty is human, all too human.

Since the concept of natural aggressiveness cannot account for collective violence, maybe we should prefer that of the 'death instinct'. In coining this notion in the context of the First

World War, Freud was attempting to fathom the unfathomable, to explore the enigma of violence at its core.[2] Violence is easily explained when its instrumental character is invoked: excessive use of force aiming to produce effects of domination, astonishment, capture. But no rational goal, no Cartesian aim, could ever explain the irrational dementia of the two world wars. We can understand Freud, struck as he was by this European disaster: only invocation of an irrational instinct for putting the self to death is capable of at least indicating, without wholly explaining, the madness of wars, the rage to destroy one another.

Following this preamble, we may return to the triptych of the 'major classical causes of war', taking as our guide a canonical text by Hobbes: Chapter 13 of *Leviathan*.

The first cause, unsurprisingly, is the pursuit of material gain: seizing the assets of others, conquering land, appropriating deposits of precious metals, and so on. The pursuit of profit – greed – is allegedly the ultimate reason for wars. We recall that, at the time of the Gulf War and then afterwards in Iraq, while the media advertised noble principles of aid to oppressed peoples, of violated sovereignty, occasionally floating through public debate was some sceptical talk: What if, *in fact*, the real reason was oil? Over and above this straightforward statement (sometimes cynical but all too often realistic), we must *deepen* the 'economic cause' of wars. What often renders predation necessary is scarcity: a country lacking mineral resources will be tempted to appropriate those of its neighbour. In his *Critique of Dialectical Reason*, Sartre identified scarcity as the major culprit in interhuman violence:

given that two individuals cannot be satisfied by *one and the same* object, combat will determine its owner. Scarcity, then, but perhaps also, and above all, what inevitably leads human beings into war is the discrepancy, the discord between the limitation of our possessions and the limitlessness of our desires. And then we might refer to an 'economics of facility'. Through violence, I rapidly make myself master of goods that are the fruit of prolonged labour by others – theft has always been denounced as the temptation of the lazy. Through violence, I instantly become a property owner, even if it remains to assess the relationship between the size of the risk run and that of the time gained.

Finally, predatory wars can feed off jealousy, envy. Here we might remember some of René Girard's famous theories about mimetic violence, which deduce the inevitability of wars from the dynamics of human desire. At bottom, the appetite for an object is never pure. Only superficially do we imagine that our desire is motivated by objective qualities, as if it involved a two-way encounter: between me and the coveted object. When Girard asserts that desire is 'triangular', he is criticizing this illusion: it is always another's desire that gives the adored object its radiance and suddenly renders it so dazzling and attractive.[3] There is no great love that did not have jealousy as a powerful stimulant, leading to rivalry, and ultimately conflict. Desire is not a simple relationship between a loving subject and a lovable object, as if nature had preordained secret affinities between beings. Had it done so, the adventure of existence would consist in finding the person, places and activities conforming to one's desire. No, what fires desire for an object is to see the other who enjoys it – hence, immediate war. In the totality of these factors, so-called 'economic' causes are unavoidable. We can even find historical evidence for them here and there – for example, the thesis advanced by palae-ontologists that wars in human history began in the Neolithic.[4] That was when, following the extended period of hunter-gatherers (Palaeolithic), and with the emergence of sedentary societies structured by a responsible state, developing industry and livestock farming and so on, food reserves, tool stocks and herds were built up, and war appeared in the form of aggressive opera-tions: raids, extortion, occupation, and so forth.

The Neolithic is traditionally also understood as the time when the separation between tasks, external and household, and the division and hierarchical ranking of the sexes, became established. War reinforced the need for such divisions: it made them urgent and unavoidable. But the effect can be the secret cause. War can also represent this for human culture: the establishment of sexual difference through violence. It is not that this difference is imposed violently; but war sanctions its necessity, its urgency. In the 'normality' of wars, the separation and primacy of the masculine are invariably celebrated, restored, reinsured.

Once we have set out the thesis that war is a strategy of appro-priation by armed violence, with its effects of establishing the male, it remains to clarify the idea of appropriation. Exclusive appropriation is the assertion of a right claiming a monopoly of enjoyment over a particular object.

At first sight, the relationship between war and private prop-erty might seem entirely negative. After all, war authorizes requisition, spoliation, extortion and sequestration, all of them legitimized by a higher principle: the safety of the nation. Private property encounters its limits in raison d'état, and the state of war justifies such encroachments. But this clash is superficial. Understood as a way of appropriating territory and resources through violence, never hesitating to crush, burn and destroy, war in fact reveals the accursed part of private property. We know its luminous part: the responsible preservation of what one owns, its conservation and improvement. Its accursed part is abuse. *Jus utendi et abutendi*, as the Romans put it: property affords me a right of abuse over the object acquired. After all, Marx said, the factory boss has appropriated the worker's labour time through a contract. He abuses it by speeding up work rates and multiplying tasks to the point of bodily exhaustion. The major landowner abuses his land by demanding its maximum exploitation in order to get rich, increasing yield to the point of soil exhaustion. War abuses human beings by dispatching them to the front, wealth by making them serve enterprises of destruction, because (as Kant had already pointed out) the head of state, the prince, regards himself as the *owner* of his people.

On the more specific relationship between capitalist appropriation and war, we are familiar with the classic Marxist thesis that interstate wars are a logical consequence of imperial rivalries. Great powers are prompted to confront one another in their frantic pursuit of colonization (discovering new markets for the export of their excess output, new energy resources to operate factories, and so on). More profoundly, in a speech of 7 March 1895 French socialist Jean Jaurès declared that war between states was merely one expression of social systems which domestically encouraged violent logics of competition and rivalry in the name of 'liberal progress'. Hence his formula 'Capitalism carries within it war, just like clouds carry rain,' declaimed on 25 July 1914.

We might further invoke a third thesis, more secret and doubtless more conspiratorial in nature (here we re-encounter Erasmus's provocation, already mentioned): war between states makes it possible to *distract* populations from revolutionary movements aspiring to overthrow the property-owning elite and reintroduce the idea of the 'common' in the means of production, in public services, and in essential goods. On the announcement of major wars, we have sometimes heard the following repeated: workers, peasants, employees, this is not your battle. It is as if the secret, ultimate function of wars was to guarantee the sacrosanct right of private property, to *protect* property-owners, to perpetuate their right to abuse the world.

In Chapter 13 of *Leviathan*, Hobbes signals a second cause of war: fear. Once again, this explanation might seem self-evident: it is when a neighbouring country becomes highly threatening, when it dangerously increases its military resources, its strike capacity, that I feel entitled to respond to what I experience as provocation.

One can then speak of *anticipatory* self-defence: preventive war when the threats are multiplying; pre-emptive wars when an attack is imminent. To justify his attack on Ukraine, even Vladimir Putin brandished the spectre of danger: a resurgence of neo-Nazi movements in Ukraine and encirclement by NATO forces. Justified or feigned, fear is regularly invoked. It is the good reason, the acceptable motive, which transforms intolerable aggression into self-defence. At the same time, sticking to a clear-cut alternative between justified and feigned fear is complicated. The anticipation fed by fear leads us into an infernal spiral. For the imagination is lively. On what sound bases could I ever claim that a neighbouring state, a foreign power, has definitively renounced invading and seeking to seize our wealth? Of course, there are declarations of friendship, peace treaties, and so on. But everyone knows that the history of states is one of betrayals and volte-faces.

Every sovereign is therefore reduced to interpreting signs: troop movements, rearmament, and so on. But the imagination electrified by fear does not stop at what it can observe. Could there not be secret agreements made between powers to strangle me? What proof is there that clandestine arms purchases have not occurred? Imagination rushes to judgement, and I become mistrustful. And, faced with my disquiet, the *other* does not remain inactive. He interprets my new distrust as a tangible threat, and rearms to anticipate the perceived perils. And this preparation for battle is seen by me as confirmation of my initial intuition.

That is how enmity between individuals or wars between states break out: by cross-bred anticipations of ill intent. The intersection of two fears ends up creating a reality: the hostility which, once suspected, goes right to the end of the road of death. Mutual paranoia, which feeds off threats and fears.

Erasmus hit upon a striking formula to express the creation of conflicts by these phantoms of fear, stirred up by the imagination: 'War is born of a semblance of war.'[5]

The final root of war consists in a mental disposition that might almost be said to be the opposite of fear: 'vanity'. By it Hobbes means everything to do with the display of one's superiority, a proud self-assertion. It concerns wars – and they are numerous – that pursue a predominantly symbolic victory: occupying a site steeped in history to re-legitimize one's position, to showcase the effectiveness of one's weaponry and the superiority of one's command, to heroize the head of the armed forces.

But, to deepen this causal register, we must go beyond the idea of crowing (waging war so as to figure in the history books). It is easy to neglect or downplay this cause of war, on the grounds that it is impossible to conceive of a responsible politician engaging in such a ruinous and disastrous operation as war for frivolous motives of vainglory.

Here we must revert to Hegel's intuitions in *Phenomenology of Spirit*: any struggle for prestige is invariably a struggle to the death. The quest for recognition, or rather the fervour to demonstrate to the other that one surpasses him, presupposes the moment when I sufficiently overcome the fear of dying to prove my superiority. It is as if scorn for my merely immanent life, my ability to risk it for a noble deed, a symbolic revenge, or whatever, immediately raised me to the pinnacle. Alas, we are all too familiar with the adolescent inclination for games of rivalry and daring. But, it will be said, the leaders of great powers have gone beyond the difficult age of puberty. Historically, there are certainly very few warmongers and declarers of war who risk their lives on the battlefield. Yet it is impossible to deny the existence of wars of pure prestige.

To take the example of the Ukrainian conflict, we can see how this tripartite interpretative grid works perfectly. Greed: Russia's desire to control the breadbasket of Europe. Fear: Moscow experiences the prospect of Ukraine's membership of NATO as an intolerable threat. Prestige: as Zbigniew Brzezinski noted, Ukraine is the last bastion enabling Russia to consider itself an empire.[6]

In order to go beyond them, let us return for a moment to Hegel and his thesis on the relationship between wars and history. He sought to advance a general explanation: war is the motor of history, whereby humanity advances, progresses and realizes itself. This is an obviously paradoxical thesis, since it assumes an absolutely positive dimension to wars. That said, we can easily find examples: Rome's wars of conquest had civilizing effects, extending Roman genius (law, administration, urban art, and so on) to the far reaches of the Western world; Napoleon's imperial wars formed part of the European diffusion of revolutionary ideals.

The twentieth century invalidated these progressivist utopias, these consoling dreams (the dead served a purpose). The two world wars cannot be justified by any massive civilizing effect. It may well be thought that they precipitated certain developments (the role of women in the world of work, medical progress, and so on). But what they prompted above all was the invention and production of ever more destructive weapons.

It is nevertheless possible, I think, to make an illuminating connection between history and war, but one not inscribed in the horizon of progress. The Ukrainian conflict provides us with an immediate illustration. With its aggression, Russia is seeking to avenge the humiliation following the loss of its empire. We can thereby see that wars represent opportunities for avenging one's own history, moments of the 'return of the repressed'. In his explanatory trinity (greed, vanity and fear), Hobbes neglected a decisive passion: anger. And 'anger' is not (or not only) to be understood as a surge of rage, an instinctual outpouring, an intense emotion arising from excessive stress. As Aristotle had already clearly seen, anger is above all a desire for revenge, a desire to avenge a humiliating past, a rage turned against that past and intent on restoring a lost dignity.[7] Is not bellicose anger precisely a desperate attempt to rewrite history – the history of one's people for the leader, or one's own for the combatant? We can invoke the 'return of the repressed' to indicate that, in the violence of wars, the resolution of unresolved grievances and ancient slights is dramatized. In the civil wars that over the last decade have torn apart various Middle Eastern countries – countries organized, prior to the abrupt fall of regimes (Iraq, Syria, Yemen), by the oppression of communities for the benefit of ruling minorities – such opportunities for revenge for years of humiliation have had terrible outcomes. Bitterness is a formidable destructive energy, and we must go beyond Hegel to recognize that many wars are waged not *for* history, but *against* it.

Conclusion:
And War for the Sake of What Peace?

Wars end one day and begin again another. They are destined to stop, just as motion ends in rest, and begin again. Peculiar and often inexplicable. On the one hand, as Aristotle said, war is waged 'for peace', it is never an end in itself: 'nobody chooses to make war or provokes it for the sake of making war'.[1] For his part, Raymond Aron chose to have a rather similar sentence from Herodotus engraved on his ceremonial Académie française sword: 'No-one is mad enough to prefer war to peace.' This betokens that when people wage war, it is in order to wrest a sounder, more lasting peace, as if peace were the sole purpose of the fighting. On the other hand, we may find that peace is but a time in which to prepare for future wars, a period of calm during which warriors regain courage and armies re-form, becoming ever more powerful and murderous: an interstice between two massacres, an interval, a breathing space.

But all these formulations remain general, in that they assume peace has an unequivocal meaning, whereas it is frequently as ambiguous and diverse as that of war. Countless varieties of peace, each with its own unique style, circulate in history. I shall present some of them below.

The most ironic peace (should one appreciate black humour), the most pessimistic too, is that dubbed by Leibniz and Kant the 'peace of the graveyard'. The idea here is that war is so consubstantial with humanity that we can only attain perfect tranquillity in the thick darkness of *Thanatos*. The dead no longer fight. Wars are major stimulants of peace in that they accelerate people's precipitation into nothingness.

A less radical form of this idea might be invoked: what is called 'armed' peace. It can be construed in at least three senses. Firstly, periods of peace are genuinely 'fostered' by war, which is a laboratory, a matrix of forms, of material production or societal organization invented in wartime, set to develop, flourish and ramify in peacetime. Following this line of thought, Marx wrote, 'the new forms of material production develop through war before developing in peacetime production'.[2] The author of *Capital* was thinking predominantly of industrial modes of production, scientific inventions (work rates in the factory, pharmaceutical treatments, and so on), which increased as a result of the stimulation offered by the imperatives of war. But we can elaborate on his intuition by arguing that it is not only technological innovations, precipitated by military urgency, which are tried and tested in wartime, but also forms of social organization, surveillance and indoctrination. Did not advertising propaganda on a 'mass' scale have its origins in the entry into the war of the United States in 1917 – something that had to be 'sold' to the American people?[3]

We can speak of 'armed peace' in a second sense, already explored in the opening chapter. There I observed that, in the context of the 'global war' (2001–21) that followed the Cold War (1947–89), 'security' operations – to secure territory where the Western powers had 'intervened' to expel rulers (authoritarian, corrupt, oppressive, putative accomplices of terrorist groups) – maintained a fragile peace with difficulty. In fact, they proved more murderous than the war itself (bombings, ambushes, surprise attacks). Here, peace becomes what is *kept* by arms, and by endlessly repeated intimidation.

In a third, much broader sense, we can say that peace is always armed if we agree to invert Clausewitz's formula: politics is war continued by other means. Domestic peace and public order are only ever a thin veneer, and external war a horrible diversion. Real war, waged within states, insidious and disguised, is the one pursued by a minority against its own people in peacetime. The armed peace of real tyrannies and false democracies is that imposed on the majority by a minority, using police and taxes, labour and property laws. As revealed by both Ibn Khaldûn in his *Book of Lessons* and Rousseau in his *Discourse on Inequality*, the horrible secret of state organizations is that a bellicose minority – possessing the weapons of finance and justice, industry and public authority – wages a silent, permanent war on its own people.[4] And external wars are simply a way for the state either to reinforce this armed peace, which is organized to benefit a minority, or to conceal the fundamental division it involves – what Marx called 'class struggle'.

But what we must hope for, and what philosophy can rationally justify, are more promising, more authentic forms than armed peace or the peace of the graveyard. Without, obviously, dreaming of a millenarian peace as the end of history, some miraculous age ushered in by a 'last' colossal, monstrous war that cleanses all impure elements, we can at least advance two less mystical propositions by way of conclusion, showing that war is always anti-republican in Kant's sense and anti-democratic in Spinoza's.

In his 'First Definitive Article of a Perpetual Peace', Kant defends a fierce intuition: as long as a prince, a sovereign or a state regards itself as 'owner' of its people, it will abuse them in accordance with the logic denounced in the last chapter. It will be prepared to sacrifice them for personal ambition, ready to dispose of them for convenience's sake. Were the decision theirs, unless their safety was at stake, peoples would never be so willing to envisage 'calling down on themselves all the miseries of war'.[5] The reasoning is simple: a republic only wages war to defend itself. Hence, if all states were republics, none of them would any longer have to fear aggression from another. Peace is therefore to be anticipated from a progressive transformation of the internal constitutions of states into genuine republics.

But if peace so 'suits' humanity, as long as it is organized in accordance with a republican form, that is also because it is profoundly 'natural', in the sense the term assumes in Spinoza. Peace is natural, and what generates war is a defect of nature. To understand this, we must abandon the facile verity which has it that war between states is, alas, natural, and that it requires all the endeavour and genius of culture to establish the conditions for a lasting peace. If this opposition between bellicose nature and pacifying culture has its pedagogic virtues, it does not stand up conceptually. Adopting Spinoza's insights, we must even condemn its conceptual poverty, and regard nature as being different from a certain mode of presence of things – preserved from all cultural or civic influence: nature as the innate, the primitively given; more commonly still, as countryside and wilderness. In the fullest sense of the term, nature is to be understood as a power of composition, a principle of realization. The pianist's *natural* playing style is based on supple fingers wholly in the service of the melody. Each person's naturalness consists in the spheres where they are at the height of their powers. As we soon realize, this excludes neither apprenticeship, nor education, nor discipline: these are so many tools for perfecting nature, which is basically what *rings true*, energizes, is what powers are made of. That is why Spinoza finds it reasonably possible that a state, by means of good laws, strict education and vigilant justice will succeed in bringing 'naturalness' to people – in other words, spontaneously inspire forms of friendship and mutual aid between them, producing social harmony. Hence the idea, ultimately, that democracy is the most natural political regime, and that wars are anti-democratic: they impede and prevent a harmonious configuration of powers attesting to natural perfection.

But this solidaristic configuration is difficult to establish *between states*. The miracle of nature is difficult to realize at that level. Once again, nature is not the principle of a being's self-enclosure, it is *what is missing* from its own perfection. So, if states wage war, it is because *there is insufficient nature* between them, and too many shabby human calculations, petty ambitions, expectations harboured by limited imaginations. It is our whole culture of malicious hatred and revenge, virulent fear and arrogance, that keeps us on the verge of peace, which is the triumph of joy over the sad passions.

Notes

Introduction: This Time, It Really *Is* War

1 Timothy Snyder, *Bloodlands: Europe between Hitler and Stalin* (New York: Basic Books, 2010).

2 Here I take up a conceptual trio already formalized in my *States of Violence: An Essay on the End of War* (Calcutta: Seagull, 2010).

3 An expression and doctrine coined by General Colin Powell to illustrate the imperative of novel Western military interventions, employing ultra-modern military technology to obtain victory by making combat impossible through the paralyzing neutralization of enemy armies.

4 Alberico Gentili, *De jure belli* (1597), Book I, Chapter 2: 'Armorum publicorum justa contentio est.'

1. A *Real* 'Return' to War? Binary Wars, Global Wars, Chaos-Creating Wars

1 See, for example, Evan Luard, *The Blunted Sword: The Erosion of Military Power in Modern World Politics* (London: I.B. Tauris, 1988); John Mueller, *Retreat from Doomsday: The Obsolescence of Major War* (New York: Basic Books, 1989); Mary Kaldor, *New and Old Wars: New and Old*

Wars: Organized Violence in a Globalized Era (Palo Alto, CA: Stanford University Press, 1998); Herfried Münkler, *The New Wars*, transl. Patrick Camiller (Cambridge: Polity, 2005); Gros, *States of Violence*.

2 *Dictionnaire de Trévoux* (1704–71); Immanuel Kant, *The Philosophy of Law*, Part II, §56, transl. W. Hastie (Edinburgh: T. & T. Clark, 1887), p. 218.

3 Claude Le Borgne, *La Guerre est morte* (Paris: Grasset, 1987).

4 Georges-Henri Soutou, *La Guerre de cinquante ans (1943–1990)* (Paris: Fayard, 2001). See also André Fontaine, *History of the Cold War: From the Korean War to the Present*, 2 vols, transl. Renaud Bruce (New York: Pantheon, 1968).

5 Roger Trinquier, *La Guerre moderne* (Paris: Economica, 2008 [1961]).

6 Francis Fukuyama, *The End of History and the Last Man* (New York: Free Press, 1992).

7 For a synthesis, see Marc Hecker and Élie Tenenbaum, *La Guerre de vingt ans. Djihadisme et contre-terrorisme au XXIe siècle* (Paris: Robert Laffont, 2021).

8 Carl Schmitt, *Theory of the Partisan: Intermediate Commentary on the Concept of the Political*, transl. G. L. Ulmen (New York: Telos, 2007 [1963]).

9 On this doctrine, see Hecker and Tenenbaum, *La Guerre de vingt ans*, p. 143f.

10 This term, first used by Ronald Reagan in connection with Libya, refers to corrupt, anti-democratic states representing a threat to collective security and American interests. Jacques Derrida analyses the concept philosophically in *Rogues: Two Essays on Reason*, transl. Pascale-Anne Brault and Michael Naas (Stanford, CA: Stanford University Press, 2005).

11 Pierre Hassner, *La Terreur et l'Empire. La violence et la paix*, vol. 2 (Paris: Éditions du Seuil, 2003).

12 Petraeus was taking up the theses of David Galula, *Counterinsurgency Warfare: Theory and Practice* (Westport, CT: Praeger Security International, 1964).

13 Roland Marchal and Pierre Hassner, eds, *Guerres et sociétés. État et violence après la guerre froide* (Paris: Karthala, 2003), p. 7.

14 My characterization of them is based on my reading of Hamit Bozarslan, *Le Temps des monstres. Le monde arabe, 2011–2021* (Paris: La Découverte,

2022); Pierre-Jean Luizard, *Le Piège Daech. L'État islamique ou le retour de l'Histoire* (Paris: La Découverte, 2015) and *Les Racines du chaos. Irak, Syrie, Liban, Yémen, Libye* (Paris: Tallandier, 2022); Jean-Pierre Filiu, *Apocalyse in Islam*, transl. M. B. DeBevoise (Berkeley/Los Angeles, CA: University of California Press, 2012) and *Le Milieu des mondes. Une histoire laïque du Moyen-Orient de 395 à nos jours* (Paris: Éditions du Seuil, 2021); and Gilles Kepel, *Away from Chaos: The Middle East and the Challenge to the West*, transl. Henry Randolph (New York: Columbia University Press, 2023).

2. Heroism and Barbarism

1 'Per fare la guerra con successo, tre cose sono assolutamente necessarie: primo, il denaro, secondo il denaro, e terzo il denaro.'

2 Such is Nietzsche's thesis: 'War is another thing. I am by nature warlike. To attack is among my instincts. *To be able* to be an enemy, to be an enemy – that perhaps presupposes a strong nature, it is in any event a condition of every strong nature. It needs resistances, consequently it *seeks* resistances: the *aggressive* pathos belongs as necessarily to strength as the feeling of vengefulness and vindictiveness does to weakness. Woman, for example, is vengeful: that is conditioned by her weakness, just as is her susceptibility to others' distress. – The strength of one who attacks has in the opposition he needs a kind *of gauge*; every growth reveals itself in the seeking out of a powerful opponent – or problem: for a philosopher who is warlike also challenges problems to a duel. The undertaking is to master, *not* any resistances that happen to present themselves, but those against which one has to bring all one's strength, suppleness and mastery of weapons – to master *equal* opponents . . . Equality in face of the enemy – first presupposition of an *honest* duel. Where one despises one *cannot* wage war; where one commands, where one sees something as beneath one, one *has* not to wage war.' Friedrich Nietzsche, 'Why I am So Wise', in *Ecce Homo*, transl. Anthony M. Ludovici (New York: Dover, 2004), p. 21.

3 Jean de Bueil, *Le Jouvencel* (Geneva: Slatkine, 1996), vol. 2, p. 21; Ernst Jünger, *La Guerre comme expérience intérieure*, transl. F. Poncet (Paris: Christian Bourgois, 1977), p. 90.

4 For a full description, see Marcel Détienne, 'La phalange: problèmes et controverses', in *Problèmes de la guerre en Gréce ancienne*, ed. Jean-Pierre Vernant (Paris: Mouton, 1968).

5 Plato, *Apology of Socrates*, 28d–29a.

6 Thomas Aquinas, *Summa Theologica*, question 123, art. 6.

7 '[T]here is a victory and defeat – the first and best of victories, the lowest and worst of defeats – which each man gains or sustains at the hands, not of another, but of himself; this shows that there is a war against ourselves going on within every one of us'. Plato, *The Laws* I, transl. Benjamin Jowett (New York: Cosimo, 2008), p. 11.

8 'In order not to let them [those systems which tend to isolate themselves] become rooted and set in this isolation, thereby breaking up the whole and letting the [communal] spirit evaporate, government has from time to time to shake them to their core by war. By this means the government upsets their established order, and violates their right to independence, while the individuals who, absorbed in their own way of life, break loose from the whole and strive after the inviolable independence and security of the person, are made to feel in the task laid on them their lord and master, death.' G. W. F. Hegel, *Phenomenology of Spirit*, transl. A. V. Miller (Oxford: Oxford University Press, 1977), pp. 272–3.

9 In his *Les Guerres modernes* (Paris: Buchet-Chastel, 2009), Pierre Servent does not avoid the subject, providing several examples of these egregious furies in his chapter on 'brutalization'.

10 See also in my *States of Violence: An Essay on the End of War* (Calcutta: Seagull, 2010), in the chapter titled 'Moral Forces'.

3. What Is a 'Just' War?

1 On this subject, readers are referred, inter alia, to Alfred Vanderpol, *La Doctrine scolastique du droit de guerre* (Paris: Pédone, 1925); Peter Haggenmacher, *Grotius et la doctrine de la guerre juste* (Geneva: Publications de l'Institut, 1983); Monique Canto-Sperber, *Le Bien, la guerre et la terreur* (Paris: Plon, 2005); and Thomas Berns, *La Guerre des philosophes* (Paris: Presses Universitaires de France, 2019).

2 Saint Ambrose, *De Officiis*, I, 36, 178.

3 See, for example, Saint Augustine, *The City of God*, Book XIX, Chapter 7, transl. Henry Bettenson (London: Penguin, 2003).

4 'It may happen that, even if the authority of the one declaring war is legitimate and the cause just, the war is rendered unlawful by a wicked intention.' Thomas Aquinas, *Summa Theologica*, II, II, 40, transl. V. Vergriete O. P. (Paris: Éditions du Cerf, 1957), p. 120.

5 Francisco de Vitoria, 'On the Law of War', transl. Jeremy Lawrance, in *Political Writings*, eds. Anthony Pagden and Jeremy Lawrance (Cambridge: Cambridge University Press, 1991), p. 305.

6 'Cajetan concluded that, for a war to be just, the Prince had to recognize such power in himself that he was morally certain of victory.' Francisco Suarez, *De Bello*, quoted in Vanderpol, *La Doctrine scolastique*, p. 384.

7 'We must also know, that Kings, and those who are invested with a power equal to that of Kings, have a Right to exact Punishments, not only for Injuries committed against themselves, or their Subjects, but likewise, for those which do not peculiarly concern them, but which are, in any Persons whatsoever, grievous Violations of the Law of Nature or Nations. For the Liberty of consulting the Benefit of human Society, by Punishments, which at first, as we have said, was in every particular Person, does now, since Civil Societies, and Courts of Justice, have been instituted, reside in those who are possessed of the supreme Power, and that properly, not as they have an Authority over others, but as they are in subjection to none.' Hugo Grotius, *The Rights of Peace and War*, 3 vols, ed. Richard Tuck (Indianapolis, IN: Liberty Fund, 2005), Vol. 2, p. 1,021.

8 By this is meant the new world born after the signature of the Treaty of Westphalia, which put an end to the Thirty Years' War in Europe and laid the bases for an international system comprising equal sovereign states.

9 The expression is found in Hugo Grotius (*The Rights of Peace and War*) and Samuel Pufendorf (*On the Duty of Man and Citizen According to Natural Law*).

10 We find this expression in Emer de Vattel (*The Law of Nations*, 1758) and Christian Wolff (*Principles of the Law of Nature and Nations*, 1758).

11 Immanuel Kant, *The Philosophy of Law*, transl. W. Hastie (Edinburgh: T. & T. Clark, 1887), Pt. II, §57, p. 219.

12 Michel Foucault, *'Society Must be Defended'*, transl. David Macey (New York: Picador, 2003), p. 50.

13 Georges Duby, *Le Dimanche de Bouvines* (Paris: Gallimard, 1985 [1973]).

14 See Christine Boutin, 'L'histoire mondiale est le tribunal du monde', in *Hegel penseur du droit* (Paris: CNRS Philosophie, 2004), pp. 263–77.

15 Immanuel Kant, 'A Perpetual Peace: A Philosophical Sketch', I, 6, in *Political Writings*, ed. H. S. Reiss, transl. H. B. Nisbet (Cambridge: Cambridge University Press, 1991), p. 96.

16 See also in my *States of Violence*, in the chapter titled 'Moral Forces'.

4. The State Makes War and War Makes the State

1 Jean-Jacques Rousseau, 'The Social Contract', I, 4, in *The Social Contract and Other Later Political Writings*, ed. and transl. Victor Gourevitch (Cambridge: Cambridge University Press, 1997), p. 46.

2 On this comparison, see Judith E. Schlanger, *Les Métaphores de l'organisme* (Paris: Vrin, 1971).

3 The theses of social Darwinism were ideologically decisive in facilitating the outbreak of the First World War. See Thomas Lindemann, *Les Doctrines darwiniennes et la guerre de 1914* (Paris: Economica, 2001).

4 Carl Schmitt, *Ex captivitate salus: Expériences des années 1945–1947*, transl. A. Doremus (Paris: Vrin 2003). [This sentence does not feature in the English translation published by Polity in 2017. Trs.]

5 Carl Schmitt, *The Concept of the Political*, transl. George Schwab (Chicago/London: University of Chicago Press, 2007), p. 26.

6 'Whoever does not increase decreases when others increase. It is perfectly possible for a private man to say: "I am satisfied and wish for nothing more." . . . A state that engages in this practice of humble moderation would have to be either highly favoured by its situation, or unattractive prey, for it not to rapidly lose what it humbly contented itself with, and for it not to find that the words "I wish for nothing more" actually had this meaning: "there is absolutely nothing I want, I do not even wish to exist".' Johann Gottlieb Fichte, *Sur Machiavel écrivain*, transl. L. Ferry and A. Renaut (Paris: Payot, 1981).

7 'For as the nature of Foule weather, lyeth not in a showre or two of rain; but in an inclination thereto of many dayes together: So the nature of War, consisteth not in actuall fighting; but in the known disposition

thereto, during all the time there is no assurance to the contrary. All other time is PEACE.' Thomas Hobbes, *Leviathan*, ed. Richard Tuck (Cambridge: Cambridge University Press, 1996), pp. 88–9.

8 Ibid., p. 90.

9 'There is no other means of cleansing Republics of such ordure than sending them off to war, which is like a purgative medicine and highly necessary for expelling the corrupted humours from the universal body of the Republic. War on the enemy is a way of preserving friendship between subjects.' Jean Bodin, *Les Six Livres de la République*, Book V, Chapter 5 (Paris: Fayard, 1993).

10 Niccolò Machiavelli, *The Discourses*, Book III, Chapter 16, transl. Leslie J. Walker, ed. Bernard Crick (London: Penguin, 1998), pp. 451–3.

11 Erasmus, *The Complaint of Peace* (Chicago/London: Open Court, 1917), p. 32.

12 See his commentary in *The City and Man* (Chicago: Rand McNally, 1964). Thucydides' dialogue is to be found in Book V, Chapter 105 of *The War of the Peloponnesians and the Athenians*, ed. and transl. Jeremy Mynott (Cambridge: Cambridge University Press, 2013), pp. 382–3.

13 On their role, see Nicole Loraux, *The Invention of Athens: The Funeral Oration in the Classical City* (Princeton, NJ: Princeton University Press, 2006).

14 'A ruler, then, should have no other objective, and no other concern, nor occupy himself with anything else except war and its methods and practices.' Niccolò Machiavelli, *The Prince*, eds. Quentin Skinner and Russell Price, transl. Russell Price (Cambridge: Cambridge University Press, 1988), pp. 51–2.

15 See also in my *States of Violence*, in the chapter titled 'Political Stakes'.

5. The Idea of Total War

1 Léon Daudet, *La Guerre totale* (Paris: Nouvelle Librairie nationale, 1918); Erich Ludendorff, *Der Totale Krieg*, translated into English as *The 'Total' War* (London: Friends of Europe, 1936).

2 Comte de Guibert, *Stratégiques* (Paris: L'Herne, 1977), p. 613.

3 Essentially in Carl Schmitt, *The* Nomos *of the Earth in the International*

Law of the Jus Publicum Europaeum, transl. G. L. Ulmen (Candor, NY: Telos, 2003 [1950]).

4 Jean-Jacques Rousseau, 'The Social Contract', I, 4, in *The Social Contract and Other Later Political Writings*, ed. and transl. Victor Gourevitch (Cambridge: Cambridge University Press, 1997), p. 46. My emphasis.

5 Ernst Jünger, 'Total Mobilization', in *The Heidegger Controversy: A Critical Reader*, ed. Richard Wohlin, transl. Joel Golb and Richard Wohlin (Cambridge, MA: MIT Press, 1993).

6 Niccolò Machiavelli, *The Discourses*, Book II, Chapter 8, ed. Bernard Crick, transl. Leslie J. Walker (London: Penguin, 1998), pp. 294–5.

7 Hannah Arendt, *The Origins of Totalitarianism* (New York: Houghton Mifflin Harcourt, 1951).

8 Martin Heidegger, *The Question Concerning Technology and Other Essays*, transl. William Lovitt (New York/London: Garland, 1977 [1953]).

9 Quoted in Carl von Clausewitz, *On War*, eds. and transl. Michael Howard and Peter Paret (London: Everyman, 1993), p. 7.

10 See also in my *States of Violence* in the Conclusion.

6. Why War?

1 Konrad Lorenz, *On Aggression*, transl. Marjorie Kerr Wilson (London: Methuen, London 1966 [1963]).

2 See Sigmund Freud, 'Beyond the Pleasure Principle' (1920), in *The Standard Edition of the Complete Psychological Works of Sigmund Freud*, Vol. XVIII (1920–22), transl. James Strachey et al. (London: Vintage, 2001), but also Freud's letter to Albert Einstein, 'Why War?' (1932), in *The Standard Edition of the Complete Psychological Works*, Vol. XXII (1932–36), transl. James Strachey et al. (London: Vintage, 2001).

3 See René Girard, *Deceit, Desire and the Novel: Self and Other in Literary Structure*, transl. Yvonne Freccero (Baltimore, MD: Johns Hopkins University Press, 1966 [1961]).

4 See, for example, Jean-Paul Demoule, *Les dix millénaires oubliés qui ont fait l'histoire* (Paris: Fayard, 2017).

5 'War is sweet to those who have not waged it.' Erasmus, *guerre et paix dans la pensée d'Érasme de Rotterdam*, ed. Jean-Claude Margolin (Paris: Aubier-Montaigne, 1973), p. 117.

6 See Zbigniew Brzezinkski, *The Grand Chessboard: American Primacy and Its Geostrategic Imperatives*, new edn (New York: Basic Books, 2016 [1997]).

7 Aristotle, *Rhetoric*, Book II, 1378b.

Conclusion: And War for the Sake of What Peace . . .

1 Aristotle, *Ethics*, Book Ten, 1177b7–12, transl. J. A. K. Thomson (Harmondsworth: Penguin, 1976), p. 329.

2 Quoted in Karl Korsch, *Marxisme et contre-révolution* (Paris: Éditions du Seuil, 1975), p. 230.

3 On this, see David Colon, *Propagande. La manipulation de masse dans le monde contemporain* (Paris: Belin, 2019).

4 Compare Gabriel Martinez-Gros's presentation of it in his *Brève histoire des empires* (Paris: Éditions du Seuil, 2014).

5 Immanuel Kant, 'Perpetual Peace: A Philosophical Sketch', in *Political Writings*, ed. Hans Reiss, transl. H. B. Nisbet (Cambridge: Cambridge University Press, 1991), p. 100.